Brief Contents

W9-AXI-380

 LearningCurve activity is available for this topic. Visit **bedfordstmartins.com/rsinteractive**.

Real
Skills
INTERACTIVE

Real Skills

INTERACTIVE

A Brief Guide to Writing Sentences and Paragraphs

Susan Anker

Bedford / St. Martin's
Boston ◆ New York

For Bedford / St. Martin's

Publisher for College Success and Developmental Studies: Edwin Hill
Executive Editor for Developmental Studies: Alexis Walker
Developmental Editor: Jill Gallagher
Senior Production Editor: Bridget Leahy
Senior Production Supervisor: Dennis Conroy
Marketing Manager: Christina Shea
Copy Editor: Steve Patterson
Indexer: Melanie Belkin
Senior Art Director: Anna Palchik
Text Design: Claire Seng-Niemoller
Cover Design: Billy Boardman
Composition: Graphic World Inc.
Printing and Binding: RR Donnelley and Sons

President, Bedford/St. Martin's: Denise B. Wydra
Editorial Director for English and Music: Karen S. Henry
Director of Development: Erica T. Appel
Director of Marketing: Karen R. Soeltz
Production Director: Susan W. Brown
Director of Rights and Permissions: Hilary Newman

Manufactured in the United States of America.

8   7   6   5   4   3
f   e   d   c   b   a

For information, write: Bedford / St. Martin's, 75 Arlington Street, Boston, MA 02116
(617-399-4000)

ISBN 978-1-4576-5410-7

Acknowledgments

Acknowledgments and copyrights are continued at the back of the book on page 234, which constitutes an extension of the copyright page. It is a violation of the law to reproduce these selections by any means whatsoever without the written permission of the copyright holder.

Contents

Part Three
Grammar, Punctuation, and Mechanics

 LearningCurve activity is available for this topic. Visit **bedfordstmartins.com/rsinteractive.**

☑️ **LearningCurve activity is available for this topic. Visit bedfordstmartins.com/rsinteractive.**

Preface

Real Skills Interactive has a two-fold goal: to show students that writing is essential to success in the real world and to help them develop the skills they need to achieve that success in their own college, work, and everyday lives. It began with a question that dogged my teaching, my travels, and my candid conversations with students and instructors around the country: How can we as educators help students more fully see that writing will open doors and that, whatever students' chosen fields, they will need to be able to write clearly and correctly? How can we place sentence- and paragraph-level skills in the large and compelling context of the real world?

In a brief, affordable format, *Real Skills Interactive* (like *Real Writing Interactive* and *Real Essays Interactive*) addresses these questions with core features that connect the writing class to students' other courses, to their real lives, and to the expectations of the larger world, and with a new interactive format that brings grammar practice to life via LearningCurve, a game-like, adaptive quizzing system that helps students learn as they go.

Core Features

- **Brief, Affordable Format.** The text offers what's essential for the sentence-to-paragraph level course—process-oriented writing instruction and focused grammar lessons—in a concise and affordable format.

- ✓ **Interactive Grammar Practice via LearningCurve.** LearningCurve's innovative adaptive online quizzing lets students learn at their own pace, and a game-like interface encourages them to keep at it. Quizzes are keyed to grammar instruction in the book, so what is taught in class gets reinforced at home. Instructors can also check in on each student's activity in a grade book.

  A student access code is printed in every new student copy of *Real Skills Interactive*. Students who do not buy a new print book or e-book can purchase access by going to **bedfordstmartins.com/rsinteractive**. Instructors can also get access at this site.

  NOTE: LearningCurve is also available in WritingClass or SkillsClass, so if you're using either Class, encourage your students to use it there.

- **Real-World Examples.** Samples of real students' writing demonstrate the concepts covered and give students confidence that good writing skills are achievable. A focus on real-life correspondence, such as e-mails and cover letters, help students connect writing to their everyday lives.

- **Four Basics Boxes.** Presenting writing skills in manageable increments, these boxes break down the essentials of topics such as revision, good paragraphs, and narration.

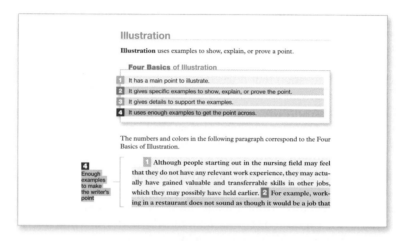

- **Focus on the Four Most Serious Errors.** *Real Skills Interactive* concentrates first on the four types of grammatical errors that matter most: fragments, run-ons, errors in subject-verb agreement, and errors of verb tense and form. Once students master these four topics and start building their editing skills, they are better prepared to tackle the grammar errors treated in later chapters.

You Get More with *Real Skills Interactive*

Real Skills Interactive does not stop with a book. Online, you will find more resources to help students get even more out of the book and your course. You will also find free, convenient instructor resources, such as a downloadable instructor's manual.

For more information, visit **bedfordstmartins.com/rsinteractive /catalog**.

STUDENT RESOURCES

Premium Resources

- **WritingClass** provides students with a dynamic, interactive online course space preloaded with exercises, diagnostics, video tutorials, writing and commenting tools, and more. WritingClass helps students stay focused and lets instructors see how they are progressing. It is available at a significant discount when packaged with the print text. To learn more about WritingClass, visit **yourwritingclass.com**.

- **SkillsClass** offers all that WritingClass offers, plus guidance and practice in reading and study skills. This interactive online course space comes preloaded with exercises, diagnostics, video tutorials, writing and commenting tools, and more. It is available at a significant discount when packaged with the print text. To learn more about SkillsClass, visit **yourskillsclass.com**.

- *Re:Writing Plus*, **now with VideoCentral,** gathers all of our premium digital content for the writing class into one online collection. This impressive resource includes innovative and interactive help with writing a paragraph; tutorials and practices that show how writing works in students' real-world experience; VideoCentral, with more than 140 brief videos for the writing classroom; the first ever peer-review game, *Peer Factor*; *i-cite: visualizing sources*; plus hundreds of models of writing and hundreds of readings. *Re:Writing Plus* can be purchased separately or packaged with *Real Skills Interactive* at a significant discount.

Free* with the Print Text

- The *Bedford/St. Martin's ESL Workbook* includes a broad range of exercises covering grammatical issues for multilingual students of varying language skills and backgrounds. Answers are at the back. ISBN: 978-0-312-54034-0

- The *Make-a-Paragraph Kit* is a fun, interactive CD-ROM that teaches students about paragraph development. It also contains exercises to help students build their own paragraphs, audio-visual tutorials on four of the most common errors for basic writers, and the content from *Exercise Central to Go: Writing and Grammar Practices for Basic Writers*. ISBN: 978-0-312-45332-9

- The *Bedford/St. Martin's Planner* includes everything that students need to plan and use their time effectively, with advice on preparing schedules and to-do lists plus blank schedules and calendars (monthly and weekly). The planner fits easily into a backpack or purse, so students can take it anywhere. ISBN: 978-0-312-57447-5
    *NOTE: There is a limit of one free supplement per order. Additional supplements can be packaged at a significant discount.

e-Book Options

- *Real Skills Interactive* e-book. Available as a value-priced e-book, either as a CourseSmart e-book or in formats for use with computers, tablets, and e-readers—visit **bedfordstmartins.com/rsinteractive /catalog** for more information.

INSTRUCTOR RESOURCES

- ■ *Practical Suggestions for Teaching Real Skills Interactive* provides helpful information and advice on teaching developmental writing. It includes sample syllabi, tips on building students' critical thinking skills, resources for teaching nonnative English speakers and speakers of nonstandard English dialects, ideas for assessing students' writing and progress, and up-to-date suggestions for using technology in the writing classroom and lab. To download, see **bedfordstmartins.com/rsinteractive/catalog**.

- ■ *Additional Resources for Teaching Real Skills Interactive* is a collection of resources that supplements the instructional materials in the text. It contains a variety of extra exercises and tests, transparency masters, planning forms, and other reproducibles for classroom use. To download, see **bedfordstmartins.com/rsinteractive/catalog**.

- ■ *Answer Key for Real Skills Interactive* contains answers to the practice exercises in the printed book. To download, see **bedfordstmartins.com/rsinteractive/catalog**.

Acknowledgments

As with the rest of the Anker series, *Real Skills Interactive* grew out of a collaboration with teachers and students across the country and with the talented staff of Bedford / St. Martin's. I am grateful for everyone's thoughtful contributions.

REVIEWERS

I would like to thank the following instructors for their many good ideas and suggestions for this edition. Their insights were invaluable.

Nikki Aitken, Illinois Central College
Valerie Badgett, Lon Morris College
Michael Briggs, East Tennessee State University
Andrew Cavanaugh, University of Maryland University College
Jeff Kosse, Iowa Western Community College
Mimi Leonard, Wytheville Community College
Shannon McCann, Suffolk Community College
Loren Mitchell, Hawaii Community College
Jim McKeown, McLennan Community College
Virginia Nugent, Miami Dade College
Lisa Oldaker Palmer, Quinsigamond Community College
Anne Marie Prendergast, Bergen Community College
Gina Schochenmaier, Iowa Western Community College
Karen Taylor, Belmont College
Elizabeth Wurz, College of Coastal Georgia
Svetlana Zhuravlova, Lakeland Community College

A Note to Students from Susan Anker

For the last twenty years or so, I have traveled the country talking to students about their goals and, more important, about the challenges they face on the way to achieving those goals. Students always tell me that they want good jobs and that they need a college degree to get those jobs. I designed *Real Skills Interactive* with those goals in mind—strengthening the writing, reading, and editing skills needed for success in college, at work, and in everyday life.

Here is something else: Good jobs require not only a college degree but also a college education—knowing not only how to read and write but how to think critically and learn effectively. So that is what I stress here, too. It is worth facing the challenges. All my best wishes to you, in this course and in all your future endeavors.

Reading and Critical Thinking

Keys to Successful Writing

Recognize What You Already Know

You practice some form of **reading**, **critical thinking**, and **writing** every day without even realizing it. When you read advertisements, e-mails, and even bumper stickers, you often think critically about what is being presented. You question how persuasive or effective a point is. You consider how the new point fits or conflicts with what you know already (from your own experience and from other things you have read or heard). This questioning attitude and the ability to look at new material from fresh and skeptical perspectives are important building blocks for successful academic writing.

In addition to thinking critically and questioning new material, you also make decisions all the time. You think about whatever information is available to you, and you decide what to do. The more thoughtful you are about your choices, the better decisions you will make. For example, you may be considering driving yourself to school or work rather than taking public transportation. At first, it may seem like an easy choice to have your own car with you, but answer these questions:

- How much will driving cost, when you total up parking fees, gas, and additional mileage on your car?
- Are the parking-lot locations just as convenient as the transportation stations?
- If you drive, will you be giving up time you could use for reading or studying on the bus or train?

As these questions indicate, making decisions often involves weighing several factors.

LearningCurve For extra practice in the skills covered in this chapter, visit
bedfordstmartins.com/rsinteractive.

1

PRACTICE 1

Think of a decision you made recently when you had a choice about something. Maybe you started making coffee at home instead of buying it at a coffee shop to save money. Maybe you decided to work less so you could attend school. Maybe you bought a new computer or became a vegetarian.

1.   What decision did you make?

2.   What options did you have?

3.   What points did you consider to arrive at your choice?

4.   Do you think you made the right decision? Why or why not?

Careful reading and thinking lead not only to better decision making but also to better writing, both in college and at work. The next two sections talk about ways to improve the reading and thinking skills you already have in order to become a better writer.

Improve Your Critical Reading Skills

When you read for college, get in the habit of taking the following four steps, no matter what you are reading. In this section of the book, the four steps of the critical reading process are identified with the letters **2PR**.

2PR   The Critical Reading Process

Preview the reading.

Read the piece, finding the main point and support.

Pause to think during reading. Ask yourself questions about what you are reading. Imagine that you are talking to the author.

Review the reading, your notes, and your questions. Build your vocabulary by looking up any unfamiliar words.

CRITICAL READING
■ **Preview**
■ Read
■ Pause
■ Review

2PR   Preview the Reading

Before you begin to read, look ahead. Go quickly through whatever you are reading (essay, chapter, article, and so on) to get an idea of what it contains. Many books, especially textbooks, help you figure out what is important by using headings (separate lines in larger type, like "Preview the Reading" above). They may also have words in **boldface**. In textbooks, magazines, and journals, important words may be defined in the margin, or quotations may be pulled out in larger type. When you are reading a textbook or an essay or article in a college course, look through the chapter or piece for headings, boldface type, definitions in the margin, and quotations.

2PR Read the Piece, Finding the Main Point and Support

CRITICAL READING
■ **Preview**
■ **Read**
■ Pause
■ Review

Identifying the main point and support in a reading is necessary to understand the author's message.

MAIN POINT

The **main point** of a reading is the major message that the writer wants you to understand. In an advertisement or a tweet, the main point is usually easy to determine. In a longer reading, you might have to think deeply about what the main point is. It may not be lying on the surface, stated clearly and easy to spot. But in most readings, the main point is introduced early, so read the first few sentences (of a short reading) or paragraphs (of a longer reading) with special care. If the writer has stated the main point in a single sentence or a couple of sentences, highlight or double-underline those. You will remember the main point better if you write it in your own words, in either your notes or the margin of the reading.

The particular combination of skill and luck necessary to succeed at poker (especially the no-limit "Texas hold 'em" variation that's now dominant[1]) helps explain why it, rather than some other game, has become such a seminal[2] feature of the online-gambling scene. Hold 'em requires more skill than most casino games, such as blackjack and slots. The more time you put into the game, the better you get, and because skilled players do, in fact, win more money than unskilled players, there's a motivation to keep playing and learning. But poker also involves enough chance, unlike a pure-skill game like chess, so that if you play reasonably well you can get lucky enough to win a big tournament. Unlike slots, for instance, poker is an inherently[3] social and competitive game, with players up against one another rather than the house.

[1]**dominant:** most common

[2]**seminal:** important

[3]**inherently:** basically; by nature

PRACTICE 2

Read the paragraph that follows and double-underline or highlight the main point.

Your career as a health-care professional will give you much more than a steady job. You will have the satisfaction of using technical skills to help people. Whether your work involves helping children or adults, you will enjoy the respect and confidence that your training bestows.[1] Allied professionals will be very much in demand through this year and the next several years. Careers such as dental assistants, medical assistants, pharmacy technicians, medical secretaries, phlebotomy[2] technicians, and professional coders are open to you. You might perform tests, handle records and materials for dental and medical tests, assist in procedures, and learn how to use the medical or dental technical equipment. Every day can be challenging and different for you because no two patients are alike and neither are their treatments.

[1]bestows: grants

[2]phlebotomy: the process of drawing blood from a vein

SUPPORT

The **support** in a reading is the information that shows, explains, or proves the main point. To understand the main point fully, you need to be able to identify the support. If you highlighted the main point, use a different-colored marker to highlight the support. If you double-underlined the main point, underline the support, perhaps using a different-colored pencil. Using different colors will help you when you review the material for class, a writing assignment, or a test.

In the example below, the main point is double-underlined and the support is single-underlined.

Information technology (IT) is not just about computer science and engineering anymore. It can be applied as a tool in just about any pursuit from biology to fashion design. New applications in every field imaginable are being invented daily. Did you know, for example, that Sun Microsystems does a lot of its recruiting and marketing on Second Life,[1] and even holds virtual meetings there? IT has become mainstream, interwoven into the fabric of our lives.

[1]Second Life: an online virtual world for gaming and socializing

. . . .

PRACTICE 3

Reread the paragraph in Practice 2, and underline or highlight three sentences that directly support the main point. Then, briefly state the support in your own words.

. . . .

2PR Pause to Think

CRITICAL
READING
■ Preview
■ Read
■ Pause
■ Review

Critical reading requires you to actively think as you read, and taking notes and asking questions is a part of this process. As you pause to think about what you are reading, use check marks and other symbols and jot notes to yourself, so you can understand what you have read when you finish it (rather than having just looked at the words without thinking about their meaning and purpose). Here are some ways to take notes as you read:

- Note the main idea by highlighting it or writing it in the margin.
- Note the major support points by underlining them.
- Note ideas you do not understand with a question mark (?).
- Note ideas you agree with by placing a check mark next to them (✓).
- Note ideas that you do not agree with or that surprise you with an **X** or !.
- Note examples of an author's or expert's bias and how they seem biased.
- Pause to consider your reactions to parts of the reading and how a part or sentence relates to the main point.

2PR Review

CRITICAL
READING
■ Preview
■ Read
■ Pause
■ Review

Often, your instructor will ask you to answer questions about a reading or to write about it. To respond thoughtfully, review the reading, look at your notes, and use your critical thinking skills. In addition, look up any words from the reading that you are unfamiliar with.

REVIEW THE READING

When you have finished reading an assignment, review the parts you high-lighted or underlined and answer two questions:

TIP You may find that reading aloud improves your under-standing.

1. What point does the author want me to "get"?
2. What does he or she say to back up that point?

If you cannot answer these two questions, review the reading again. You need to know the answers to be able to participate in class discussion, do a writing assignment, take a test, or relate the reading to other ideas you are studying.

PRACTICE 4

Read the paragraphs that follow, highlighting or underlining the main point and the five sentences that most directly support the main point.

Consolidated Machinery offers excellent employee benefits, such as generous family leave programs and a menu of insurance plans. The family leave program offers paid two-week leaves to new parents, both mothers and fathers. These leaves are automatic, meaning that employees don't have to apply for them. Leave for new parents may be extended, without pay, for an additional four weeks. Employees may also apply for a one-week paid leave for a family emergency or a death in the immediate family. These leaves are part of what makes the company family-friendly.

The company also offers several insurance plans: two different HMOs[1] and several options of Blue Cross/Blue Shield. The company pays half of the insurance premiums for general health insurance. It also pays the entire cost of dental insurance for employees and their dependents. If employees would rather have child-care benefits than dental benefits, they can put the money that would have gone to dental care toward day care. These programs are expensive, but Consolidated Machinery has found that the additional costs are more than covered by employee loyalty and productivity.

[1]**HMOs:** Health Maintenance Organizations; health-care plans that restrict patients to certain doctors to save costs

BUILD YOUR VOCABULARY

One of the best ways to improve your vocabulary is to look up new words from your reading in a dictionary. Sometimes, as in many of the readings in this textbook, words that may be unfamiliar to some readers are highlighted and their meanings given at the end of the piece or in the margins. Keeping a record of new words and their definitions will further help you memorize their meanings.

In addition to keeping track of words as you go, your reading and writing will be much improved if you become familiar with commonly used academic words. The following list of words, taken from the Academic Word List, occur frequently in college-level work.

analyze	establish	occur
approach	estimate	percent
area	evident	period
assess	export	policy
assume	factor	principle
authority	finance	proceed
available	formula	process
benefit	function	require
concept	identify	research
consist	income	respond
constitute	indicate	role
context	individual	section
contract	interpret	sector
create	involve	significant
data	issue	similar
define	labor	source
derive	legal	specific
distribute	legislate	structure
economy	major	theory
environment	method	vary

Source: Averil Coxhead, "A New Academic Word List," *TESOL Quarterly* 34 (2000): 213–38, app. A, sublist 1. The entire Academic Word List is available at **victoria.ac.n2 /lals/resources/academicwordlist**.

. . . .

PRACTICE 5

Review the Academic Word List above. Look up any words you are unfamiliar with in a dictionary or on an online dictionary site.

. . . .

Think Critically

In all college courses, instructors expect you to think about the content and question it rather than just remember and repeat it. This ability to think carefully and ask questions is called **critical thinking**.

When reading about a subject in college or about an important matter at work or in your everyday life, ask questions as you read and as you think about what you have read. What does it mean—to the writer, to you, and to your experience? Be an active reader, not just a passive viewer.

Four Basic Critical Thinking Questions

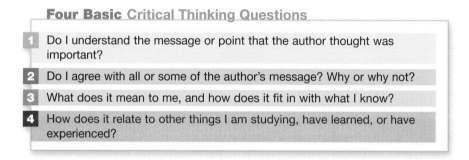

1 Do I understand the message or point that the author thought was important?

2 Do I agree with all or some of the author's message? Why or why not?

3 What does it mean to me, and how does it fit in with what I know?

4 How does it relate to other things I am studying, have learned, or have experienced?

The following text appears on the Web site for the federal government's "Let's Move" campaign and has been marked up with comments and questions that show critical thinking about the content and the message.

What's an "epidemic"?

How is this calculated?

What's the difference?

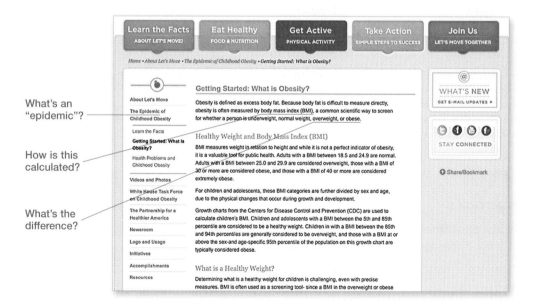

PRACTICE 6

Read the advertisement below and think about the main points it is trying to make. Note any questions or comments you have and then answer the questions that follow.

The "It's Not Like I'm Drunk" Cocktail

2 oz. tequila
1 oz. triple sec
1/2 ounce lime juice
Salt
1 too many
1 automobile
1 missed red light
1 false sense of security
1 lowered reaction time

Combine ingredients. Shake.
Have another. And another.

Never underestimate 'just a few.'
Buzzed driving is drunk driving.

Ad
Council.org

U.S. Department of Transportation

What organization is sponsoring the ad?

What does the organization want you (the reader) to do?

Was the ad successful in capturing your interest? Why or why not?

PRACTICE 7

Read the paragraphs below, which appeared in a college newspaper. Double-underline the main point sentences, and single-underline the support. Note any comments or questions you may have in the margin. Then write a paragraph in your own words using the following structure:

▪ Explain the main point in your first sentence.

▪ Explain the support in the next two or three sentences.

▪ Provide your own reaction and thoughts about the main point in the final two or three sentences.

Over 98 brands of bottled water are sold in the U.S., a country that has some of the most reliable, sanitary, and clean tap water in the world. Do we really need to be purchasing these bottles? A growing movement on college campuses nationwide claims we do not, arguing against the bottled water industry and calling on universities across the country to ban the product's sale on campuses. By replacing bottled water with public reusable-water-bottle filling stations, colleges are making it easier for students to quit their habit. We believe that [our school] should join the movement.

Those promoting the ban are correct to label disposable bottles as detrimental[1] to the environment. They produce large quantities of unnecessary waste, and reports suggest that over 68 percent of recyclable bottles are not recycled properly. Despite appearances, bottled water is often merely normal tap water that has been filtered through a process called reverse osmosis, which can require almost 10 gallons of water to purify one gallon. Such waste is simply unnecessary.

Additionally, packaging and transportation produce carbon emissions that could easily be avoided. Considering that the tap water available in our faucets is already filtered and of high quality, buying a bottle provides negligible[2] benefits while contributing to the accumulation[3] of greenhouse gases in the atmosphere. By banning the sale of bottled water on campus, [our school] could do its part to decrease these harmful emissions.

[1]**detrimental:** harmful

[2]**negligible:** barely noticeable

[3]**accumulation:** buildup

Getting Ready to Write

Writing in College and Other Formal Settings

The Basics of Good Writing

Good writing has four basic features.

Four Basics of Good Writing

1 It achieves the writer's purpose.
2 It considers the readers (the audience).
3 It includes a main point.
4 It has details that support the main point.

Purpose and Audience: Consider Your Writing Situation

Your **purpose** is your reason for writing. Your writing purpose depends on the situation. For many college writing assignments, the purpose is included within the instructions. You may be asked to show something, to explain something, or to convince someone of something. At work, your purpose in writing may be to propose something, to request something, or to summarize something. In your everyday life, your writing purpose may be to entertain or to express your feelings about something.

Closely linked to your purpose in writing is your audience. Your **audience** is the person or people who will read what you write. When you write, always have a real person in mind as a reader. In college, that person is usually your teacher, who represents the general reader. Think about what that person knows and what he or she needs to know to understand the point that you want to make.

✓ LearningCurve **For extra practice in the skills covered in this chapter, visit**
bedfordstmartins.com/rsinteractive.

PRACTICE 1

Fore each of the three writing situations below, list the purpose and audience.

1.   On Facebook, a friend posts a link to an article about bullying, and you want to write your own comment about the article and about bullying.

2.   At school, your instructor has you write a paragraph, based on some articles you have been reading and your own observations, about how bullying can affect teenagers.

3.   At work for a school district, your boss asks you to write a memo proposing a new, stronger policy against any kind of bullying on school grounds.

What you say and how you say it will vary depending on your audiences and purposes. We communicate with our friends differently than we do with people in authority, like employers or instructors. When you post a Facebook comment, you might use **informal English** because Facebook is a space for casual writing. If a friend sends you a link to a disturbing article about a bullying incident at your school, you might respond with a brief comment like this:

tx for that, hadnt seen. . . . ugh, so 2 bad u know???

In contrast, when writing a paragraph on bullying for your instructor, you would use **formal English** (with a serious tone and correct grammar and spelling) because the relationship is more formal. Also, the purpose is serious — to improve your writing skills and to achieve a good grade. You might write a passage like this:

> Bullying can have long-lasting negative effects on teenagers. When a bully picks on another student, it can hurt that person's self-esteem, in some cases permanently. If the situation is not dealt with right away, the person being bullied can spiral down into depression or even consider suicide. In some cases, bullies can cause physical harm that the person may never recover from. Some people think it is fine to look the other way when bullies pick on weaker kids, but many schools are now taking a stronger stand against bullying. New policies against bullying may save some self-esteem or even some lives.

In college, at work, and in everyday life, when you are speaking or writing to someone in authority for a serious purpose, use formal English. Otherwise, you will not achieve your purpose, whether that is to pass a course, to get and keep a good job, or to solve a personal problem (like being billed on your credit card for a purchase you did not make or reporting a landlord who does not turn on your heat). Formal English gives you power in these situations, so it is important to know how to use it. This book will give you practice in writing and speaking formal English and also in hearing it so that it sounds right to you.

Main Point and Support

Your **main point** is what you want to get across to your readers about a topic or situation. In college, instructors usually expect you to state your main point in a sentence. You may also include main-point statements in writing you do at work. Here is the main-point statement from the sample student paragraph about bullying:

> Bullying can have negative effects on teenagers.

You back up such statements by providing **support**—details that show, explain, or prove your main point. In the sample student paragraph, the support consisted of examples of the negative effects of bullying: low self-esteem, depression and suicide, physical harm. Providing enough support for your main point helps you get your ideas across and ensures that you are taken seriously.

TIP For more on main point and support, see Chapters 1 and 3.

Paragraph Structure

A **paragraph** is a short piece of writing that presents a main point and supports it. A paragraph has three parts:

1. A **topic sentence** states your main point.
2. **Body sentences** support (show, explain, or prove) your main point.
3. A **concluding sentence** reminds readers of your main point and makes an observation.

Here is an example of a paragraph:

Indentation marks start of paragraph

> Blogs (short for *Web logs*) are now an important part of many people's lives. Thousands of people write thousands of blogs on as many topics as you can think of. The topics range from cars to

Topic sentence with main point

Body
sentences
with support

entertainment to medicine to important national and international events. Many people use blogs as diaries to record their opinions, feelings, and observations. Others use blogs as a source of news instead of reading newspapers or watching television news. People visit blogs before buying things to learn what others think about certain products, features, and prices. Want to find out what others think about a movie? You can probably find any number of blogs on the subject. Blogs are a common part of our current culture, and new ones appear every minute. If you have not visited a blog, give it a try, but be careful: You might get completely hooked and become someone who writes and reads blogs every day.

Concluding
sentence

Paragraphs can be short or long, but for this course, your instructor will probably want you to have at least three to five body sentences in addition to your topic and concluding sentences. When you write a paragraph, make sure that it includes the following basic features.

Four Basics of a Good Paragraph

1 It has a topic sentence that includes the main point the writer wants to make.

2 It has detailed examples (support) that show, explain, or prove the main point.

3 It is organized logically, and the ideas are joined together so that readers can move smoothly from one idea to the next. (See Chapter 4 for more details.)

4 It has a concluding sentence that reminds readers of the main point and makes a statement about it.

The Writing Process

The following chart shows the basic steps of the **writing process**—the stages that you will move through to produce a good piece of writing. It also shows the parts of this book where you can get more information on each step.

Get Ideas
(See pages 16–19.)

• Narrow and explore your topic (prewrite).

Write
(See Chapter 3.)

- State your main point (topic sentence).
- Give details to support your point (support).
- Make an outline of your ideas (plan).
- Write a draft.

Rewrite
(See Chapter 4.)

- Reread your draft, making notes about what would make it better.
- Rewrite your draft, making changes you noted (and more).
- Reread the new draft, making sure that it is as good as you can make it.

Edit
(See Chapters 9–15.)

- Read your paper for grammar, punctuation, and spelling errors.

While you may not always go in a straight line through the four stages (you might sometimes go back to an earlier stage), it helps as a writer to have these steps in mind.

PRACTICE 2

Write a paragraph that describes an unsuccessful communication between you and someone in authority, such as a teacher, minister, returns manager at a store, or boss. You might use the following structure:

- Identify the communication situation and the participants.
- Give a few details about what each person said.
- State the outcome.
- Comment on what you might have done differently.

Narrowing and Exploring Your Topic

Narrow Your Topic

Your **topic** is what you are going to write about. Often, instructors assign a general topic that you need to make more specific so that you can write about it in a paragraph or short essay. To **narrow** a topic, break it into smaller parts that might interest you.

Patti Terwiller, a community college student in a writing class, was given an assignment to write on the general topic "A lesson that you learned." Her mind went blank. Her first thought was, "I can't think of any ideas. I don't have anything to write about on that topic." Encouraged by her teacher, she tried to narrow the general topic to a small, manageable topic (see diagram below). She also wanted to see if the narrowing process sparked any interesting ideas. First, she asked herself a question that would slightly narrow the topic. After she answered that question, she asked herself a series of questions that helped her focus on her recent experiences. Note how she keeps asking herself questions.

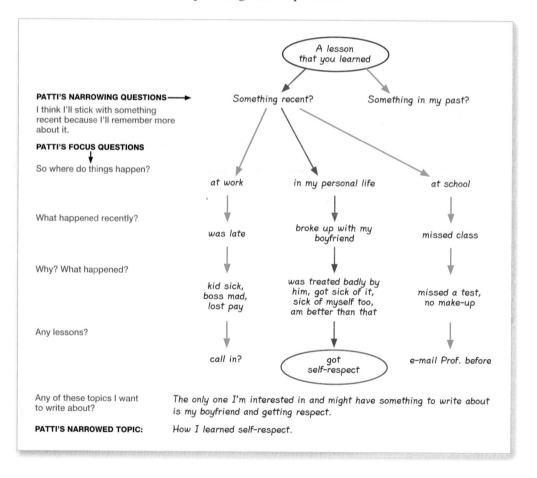

PRACTICE 3

Choose one of the following general topics, and, on a separate sheet of paper, write three narrower topics for it. Use Patti's method as a model, asking yourself a narrowing question and then a series of focusing questions. Finally, select the narrowed topic that interests you most.

A lesson that you learned	Someone that you admire
A campus problem	Something that you do well
Being a single parent	Something that you enjoy
Something that annoys you	Something that you fear
A family tradition	Stresses on students
A favorite time of day	Worries about college
A personal goal	Your best subject in school

Explore Your Topic

To get ideas to write about, use the **prewriting techniques** described in the following sections. Writers rarely use all the techniques shown here, so choose the ones that work best for you after you have tried them out. Use a prewriting technique to get ideas at any time during your writing — to narrow or explore your topic or to add details and explanations after you have begun writing a paragraph or an essay.

The examples in the rest of this chapter show Patti Terwiller, the writing student who shared her narrowing diagram, using different prewriting techniques to get ideas about the topic "A lesson that you learned." She narrowed her topic to "How I learned self-respect."

FREEWRITING

Freewriting is like having a conversation with yourself on paper. Just start writing about your topic, and continue nonstop for five minutes. Do not worry about how you write or whether your ideas are good. Just write.

> Got tired of my boyfriend pushing me around, making all the decisions, not caring what I thought. Just let it happen because I wanted to keep him. Mean to me, rude to friends, late or didn't show up. Borrowed money. At a party he started hitting on[1] someone else. Told him I had to go home. Before that, let him get away with stuff like that. He said no just wait baby. Something snapped and I got home on my own. He's history[2] and I'm kind of sad but it's okay.

[1]**hitting on:** approaching another person with romantic intentions (slang)

[2]**history:** part of the past (slang)

BRAINSTORMING

Brainstorming is listing all the ideas that you can think of without worrying about how good they are. You can brainstorm by yourself or by talking to others. Again, here is Patti Terwiller on her narrowed topic, "How I learned self-respect."

> *Always tried to please everyone, especially my boyfriends*
> *Thought everything was fine*
> *Thought love was about keeping guys happy, not myself*
> *Always got dumped anyway, couldn't figure it out*
> *Finally I just blew up, I don't really know what happened*
> *Glad it did*
> *My boyfriend was surprised, so was I*
> *He had no respect for me at all, I didn't respect myself*
> *My friends all told me but I never listened*
> *That party everything changed*
> *Never again*

Mapping or Clustering

To map, or cluster, write your narrowed topic at the top or in the center of a page. Then, write ideas about the topic that occur to you around or under your narrowed topic—anything you can think of. As details about those ideas come to you, write those around or under the ideas.

KEEPING A JOURNAL

Set aside a regular time to write in a journal. You can keep your journal on a computer or in a notebook or other small book. Write about:

- your personal thoughts and feelings,

- things that happen to you or to others, and

- things you care about but do not really understand.

Using the Internet

Do an online search using key words related to your narrowed topic. Visit some of the sites that come up, and write down any new ideas that you get about your topic.

IMPORTANT NOTE ABOUT THE INTERNET AND WRITING: The Internet is a resource for all kinds of things, including papers that you can download and turn in as your own. Doing so is called **plagiarism** and is one of the worst errors that you can make in college. Students who plagiarize may be given a failing grade automatically or may even be suspended or dismissed from college. Also, keep in mind that most instructors are expert in detecting plagiarism, and many use the Internet and software tools to check student work for originality. Do not take the risk.

PRACTICE 4

Choose two prewriting techniques and use them to explore your narrowed topic from Practice 3 (page 17). Find ideas that will be effective for both your purpose and your readers' understanding.

By now, you should have some good ideas about your narrowed topic. You will use them in the next chapters as you write your own paragraph.

PRACTICE 5

Write a first-try paragraph about your narrowed topic, using the ideas that you wrote down in the practices in this chapter. You will not be graded on this; it is a first practice. You might use the following structure:

- State your narrowed topic.

- Give the background information that the reader needs to know about the situation (who? what? when? where? why?).

- State what you learned or what is important to you about your topic, and why it is important.

3

Writing Your Paragraph

How to Put Your Ideas Together

Make a Point

Every piece of writing should have some point. Your **topic sentence** presents that point and is usually the first or the last sentence of the paragraph. Many people find that putting the topic sentence first helps them set up the rest of the paragraph. In the following paragraph, the topic sentence (main point) is underlined.

<u>Caring for my first accident victim as a student nurse was the toughest job I ever had</u>. A young mother, Serena, had been admitted to the intensive care unit after her car collided head-on with a truck. She had suffered a head injury, a collapsed lung, and a broken arm. I knew that my supervisor, a kind and highly skilled nurse, would be with me the whole time, but I was afraid. I had never assisted with a patient who was so severely injured. After Serena was wheeled into the ICU, the medical team began working on her immediately. While the doctor and senior nurses gave Serena blood and administered other care, I managed the medical pumps and kept a detailed record of everything that was being done to help her. In the end, we stabilized Serena, and my supervisor complimented me for being so calm and responsible. I will never forget how hard that time was, but it gave me confidence that I carry into every new day at work.

TIP The main point of an essay is the thesis statement. For more information, see Chapter 6.

LearningCurve For extra practice in the skills covered in this chapter, visit **bedfordstmartins.com/rsinteractive**.

One way to write a topic sentence is to use the following basic formula:

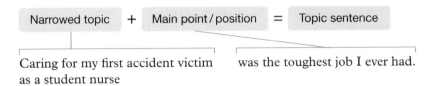

| Narrowed topic | + | Main point / position | = | Topic sentence |

Caring for my first accident victim as a student nurse   was the toughest job I ever had.

If you have trouble coming up with a main point about your topic, look back over your prewriting. For example, to write her topic sentence, Patti Terwiller, the student introduced in Chapter 2, reviewed her narrowing and prewriting about how she learned self-respect (see p. 16). She realized that the lesson that she learned through a painful experience with her boyfriend could be applied to all her relationships. Here is her topic sentence:

I finally learned self-respect in relationships.

PRACTICE 1

Reread the prewriting that you did in Chapter 2. What is the point that you want to make about your narrowed topic? Think about why the topic interests you or is important to you.

A good topic sentence has four necessary features.

Four Basics of a Good Topic Sentence

1. It has a single main point stated in a sentence.
2. It is something that you can write about in a paragraph; it is not too broad.
3. It is something that you can say something about; it is not a simple fact.
4. It is a confident statement; it is not weak and it does not start with *I think, I hope,* or *In this paper I will try to.*

TWO MAIN POINTS	Daily exercise can keep the mind alert, and eating right aids weight loss.
	[How could the writer cover these two large topics in only one paragraph?]
REVISED	Daily exercise keeps the mind alert.

TOO BROAD   Sports are popular in every culture.

[How could the writer cover this large topic in only one paragraph?]

REVISED   Baseball evolved from the British game of rounders.

SIMPLE FACT   Basketball is popular at my gym.

[What else is there to say?]

REVISED   Playing basketball has taught me the value of teamwork.

WEAK   Until students get real benefits for the activity fees they pay, I think that the college should lower these fees.

[*I think* weakens the statement.]

REVISED   Until students get real benefits for the activity fees they pay, the college should lower these fees.

PRACTICE 2

Review the Four Basics of a Good Topic Sentence on page 21. Then, read the following topic sentences and, to the left of each, write the number of the basic that is missing. Be ready to say why you chose a certain number. (More than one number may apply.)

EXAMPLE: __4__ I think that video games help people in some ways.

1. _____ Video games take mental skill, and they are coming down in price.

¹census:
a regular
population
count

2. _____ The census¹ is taken every ten years.

3. _____ There are many religions in this world.

4. _____ Fashion changes every year.

5. _____ In this paper, I hope to show that Wal-Mart hurts small businesses.

PRACTICE 3

Decide whether each of the following sentences is too broad or okay, and write **B** (broad) or **OK** in the space to the left of the sentence. Think about whether you could write a good paragraph about the sentence. Rewrite any that are too broad.

EXAMPLE: _B_ I like programs on Comedy Central.
REWRITTEN: _On Jon Stewart's The Daily Show, news is entertaining._

1. ____ People love their pets.

2. ____ Colleges offer many different kinds of degree programs.

3. ____ My grandmother saved things that most people would have thrown out.

4. ____ I love all kinds of food.

5. ____ Standardized tests are not a good measure of my abilities.

PRACTICE 4

Narrow each of the following topics. Then, circle the one that interests you most, and write a possible topic sentence for it.

EXAMPLE: Topic: Favorite pastimes
Narrowed: ____(movies)____ walking ____ cooking ____
Topic sentence: _I enjoy seeing movies because_
they take me out of my everyday life.

1. **Topic:** Things that you are good at

2. **Topic:** Benefits of an education

3. **Topic:** Difficulties that you have overcome

Here, again, is student Patti Terwiller's topic sentence:

Topic sentence: I finally learned self-respect in relationships.

After rereading her topic sentence and prewriting, Patti thought of a way to make the sentence more specific.

Revised: One evening in May, I finally learned to practice self-respect in my relationships.

PRACTICE 5

Using your narrowed topic from Chapter 2 (Practice 3, pp. 17–18) and the point that you want to make about it (Practice 1 of this chapter, p. 21), write a topic sentence. Your first try may not be perfect, so review the Four Basics of a Good Topic Sentence (p. 21), and rewrite the topic sentence to make it clearer, more specific, or more confident.

Support Your Point

A good topic sentence is important for making a main point, but it cannot stand on its own. To make sure that your writing is powerful and convincing, provide good **support**—detailed examples that show what you mean.

In the paragraph on page 20, for example, the support consists of the events that happened on the day that the student nurse cared for her first accident victim. The events show how important the day was for the writer's growth as a nurse.

Four Basics of Good Support

1 It relates to your topic sentence.

2 It tells your readers what they need to know to understand your point.

3 It uses details that show, explain, or prove your main point.

4 The details do not just repeat your main point; they explain it.

Read the following two paragraphs, which start with the same topic sentence. They were addressed to a financial aid officer by a student seeking tuition assistance.

Financial aid is key to my goal of getting a college degree. I will not have enough money to pay for tuition without financial aid. If I can get financial aid, I know that I will succeed in college. Going to college is important to me, but I will not be able to afford it unless I can get financial aid.

Financial aid is key to my goal of getting a college degree. I am the oldest of six children, and although my mother works two jobs to support us, she cannot help me with tuition. My mother did not graduate from high school, but she has always made us work hard in school so that we could go to college and have a better life. Like my mother, I have worked two jobs through high school to save for college, but they both pay the minimum wage, and my savings will not cover tuition. If I can get financial assistance, I know that I will succeed in college. Even with two jobs, I have maintained good grades. It has not been easy, but I am very motivated. I will continue to work hard, and I know from experience that hard work pays off. Financial aid will not be wasted on me.

PRACTICE 6

1. Why is the second paragraph more convincing than the first?

2. What details does the second paragraph give that the first does not?

3. What impression of the writer do you have from the first paragraph?

    From the second paragraph?

4. Why is the second paragraph more likely than the first to result in a financial aid offer?

The first paragraph does not provide support. After the topic sentence, the student simply repeats the main point using different words. The first paragraph does not contain any details explaining why financial aid is important to the student.

The second paragraph provides details that help the financial aid officer understand the writer's situation. If you put yourself in the role of the reader, you can provide support that will appeal to him or her.

The main support for a topic sentence is known as **primary support**. Good writers also provide **details** about the primary support to help readers understand the main point.

Patti Terwiller reread her prewriting and did more prewriting to get additional details about her story. Then, after rereading her topic sentence, she chose the support points that most clearly explained her main point, numbering them according to when they happened. After each point, she wrote down additional details.

> **TIP** Try prewriting to get detailed examples that support your point. See Chapter 2 for details.

> **Topic sentence:** One evening in May, I finally learned to practice self-respect in my relationships.
> **Primary support point 1:** Used to put up with[1] anything to keep my boyfriend happy.
>   **Details:** He could be late, drunk, or rude, and I'd put up with it. Could call me names around his friends or ignore me, and that was okay. I just wanted to keep him.

[1] put up with: to tolerate

> **Primary support point 2:** One night at a party, he was ignoring me as usual, but then something happened.
>   **Details:** He started making out with another girl. Something inside me snapped—knew I didn't need this.
> **Primary support point 3:** I confronted him, said it was over, and walked out.
>   **Details:** He was screaming, but I didn't look back, and I didn't answer his calls.

PRACTICE 7

First, fill in the blank in each of the following topic sentences. Then, on a separate piece of paper, write three primary support points for each sentence. Finally, pick one of the topics, and write two supporting details for each primary support point.

1. _____ is an important role model for me.

2. An important lesson I have learned is _____.

3. _____ is the most important thing in the world to me.

PRACTICE 8

On a separate sheet of paper, write your topic sentence from Practice 5 and three or four primary support points. Then, add at least two supporting details for each primary support point. Try prewriting to get ideas, and choose the ideas that show or explain your main point most effectively.

Make a Plan

Once you have your topic sentence and support points, you are ready to write, but it is easier to write if you have a plan or an outline. As you make an outline, try to shape your support into sentences.

   In the following outline, Patti turned her primary support and supporting details into complete, separate sentences. Notice also how Patti changed some of her support as she made her outline. As you write, you can change what you want to say if you come up with better ideas or words.

I. **Topic sentence:** One evening in May, I finally learned to practice self-respect in my relationships.
    A. **Support sentence 1:** I always put up with anything my boyfriend did because I was afraid he might leave me.
        1. **Details:** He was always late and drunk. I never said anything.
        2. **Details:** He never had any money, and around his friends he ignored me or was totally rude.
    B. **Support sentence 2:** At a party, he was ignoring me, as usual, but then something happened.
        1. **Details:** Right in front of me, he was coming on to[1] another girl.
        2. **Details:** I could feel something inside me snap.
    C. **Support sentence 3:** I knew I did not need this.
        1. **Details:** I told him it was over.
        2. **Details:** Then, I walked out. He was screaming, but I did not look back. I have not answered his calls.

[1]coming on to: showing romantic interest in (slang)

Sometimes, it is useful to outline writing that you have already done. This gives you a quick, visual way to see if you have too many details for one support sentence but not enough for another.

TIP For more advice on organizing your ideas, see Chapter 4.

PRACTICE 9

Write an outline of your paragraph using Patti's outline (above) as an example.

Write a Draft

Working with your outline, you are ready to write a first draft of your paragraph. Write it in complete sentences, using the details that you have developed to support your topic sentence. Include your topic sentence and a concluding sentence.

You will have as many chances as you want to make changes in your draft. The important thing now is to express your ideas in full sentences, in paragraph form.

Four Basics of a Good Draft

1 It has a topic sentence and a concluding sentence.

2 The first sentence, often the topic sentence, is indented.

3 The paragraph has complete sentences that start with capital letters.

4 It has details that show, explain, or prove the main point.

A **concluding sentence** is the last sentence in the paragraph. It reminds readers of the main point and makes a comment based on what is in the paragraph. Do not just repeat your main point.

Notice how the topic sentence and concluding sentence from the paragraph on page 20 are connected:

> **TOPIC SENTENCE:** Caring for my first accident victim as a student nurse was the toughest job I ever had.

> **CONCLUDING SENTENCE:** I will never forget how hard that time was, but it gave me confidence that I carry into every new day at work.

In her concluding sentence, the writer reminds readers that the job was difficult but makes a new point about the experience: It gave her confidence.

PRACTICE 10

Read the following two paragraphs, and write a concluding sentence for each.

1. A good mentor can mean the difference between success and failure. Fortunately for me, I found a good one in Professor Robinson. He was my English teacher during my first year in college, and without him, I would not have lasted. After four weeks of classes, I was ready to drop out. I was not doing well in my course work, and I was exhausted from working, going to class, and trying to do homework. Because he seemed to care about his students, I went up to him after class and told him that I was leaving school. I said I would try again later. Professor Robinson asked me to come to his office, where we talked for over an hour. He said that he would help me in his class and that he would arrange a meeting with my other teachers, too. He also said that I should go to the tutoring center for free extra help. He urged me to stay until the end of the semester and then decide whether to leave. I got lots of extra help from some of my teachers, and I was surprised that they were willing to spend time with me. I also made friends at the tutoring center, and we began to help each other out. I am proud to say that I stayed and passed all of my courses.

2. A career in welding offers more opportunities than you might think. Even in today's world, where so much seems to have "gone digital," many metal parts need to be put together in the physical world. Welders can work in a wide range of fields such as manufacturing, plumbing, automotive assembly and repair, construction, salvage, and mining. After some years of on-the-job experience, a welder can move up to a position as supervisor or inspector. Some experienced welders might choose to work as sales and marketing representatives,

promoting and selling specialized welding tools and equipment. In the realm of art, some metal sculptors hire welders as apprentices and studio assistants to help make their artistic visions and creations a reality, and some welders are metal sculptors themselves. Other job options in the welding field include machine technicians, metal engineers, and welding instructors.

Read Patti's draft paragraph below. Notice how Patti made changes from her outline, including the addition of a concluding sentence.

> One evening in May, I finally learned to practice self-respect in my relationships. I had always put up with anything my boyfriend did because I was afraid that he might leave me. He was always late and drunk, but I never said anything. He never had any money, and around his friends he either ignored me or was totally rude. At a party, he was ignoring me, as usual, but then something happened. Right in front of me, he was hitting on another girl. Something inside me snapped, and I knew I did not need this. I went up to him, told him our relationship was over, and walked out. He was screaming, but I did not look back. I have not answered his calls; he is history. I have learned about self-respect.

PRACTICE 11

On a separate piece of paper, write a draft paragraph. Use your outline as a guide. Feel free to make any changes that you think will improve your draft, including adding more details and changing your topic sentence or concluding sentence.

PRACTICE 12

Using some of the steps in this chapter, rewrite the first-try paragraph that you wrote at the end of Chapter 2. Once again, you will not be graded on this draft. As you reread your first-try paragraph, try to identify your main point and its primary support. Then, find places where you could add details about the support.

You might use the following format:

■   Start with a topic sentence that includes the Four Basics of a Good Topic Sentence (see p. 21).

- Make sure that you have at least three primary supports for your topic sentence.

- Add details to each primary support.

- Add one or two concluding sentences. These sentences are the last ideas of yours that your reader will read. Give your concluding sentences some extra time and thought so that they are meaningful and memorable.

4

Improving Your Paragraph

How to Make It the Best It Can Be

Understand What Revision Is

Revision means "reseeing." When you revise, you read your writing with fresh eyes and think about how to improve it. You also try to order and connect your ideas in a way that makes your meaning clear to readers.

Four Basics of Revision

1. Take a break from your draft (at least a few hours).
2. Get feedback (comments and suggestions) from someone else.
3. Improve your support, deciding what to add or drop.
4. Make sure that your ideas are ordered and connected in a way that readers will understand.

The rest of this chapter focuses on steps 2–4.

Get Feedback

Getting feedback from a reader will help you improve your first draft. Also, giving other people feedback on their writing will build your own understanding of what good writing is.

Exchanging papers with another student to comment on each other's writing is called **peer review**. Although it may feel awkward at first, that feeling will wear off as you give and get more peer review.

✓ LearningCurve For extra practice in the skills covered in this chapter, visit
bedfordstmartins.com/rsinteractive.

31

Use the following questions to get and give feedback. Although peer review may be done in writing, it is best to work face-to-face with your partner so that you can discuss each other's comments and ask questions.

CHECKLIST

Questions for a peer reviewer

☐ Is the writing style appropriate for the audience and purpose? (Most college assignments should be written in formal English.)

☐ What is the main point (topic sentence)?

☐ Is the topic sentence focused on a single topic, narrow enough for a paragraph, more than just a simple fact, and confident (without *I think* or *I hope*)?

☐ Is there enough support for the main point? Where could there be more support?

☐ Do any parts seem unrelated to the main point?

☐ Are there places where you have to stop and reread something to understand it? If so, where?

☐ Could the concluding sentence be more forceful?

☐ What do you like best about the paper?

☐ Where could the paper be better? What improvements would you make if it were your paper?

☐ If you were getting a grade on this paper, would you turn it in as is?

☐ What other comments or suggestions do you have?

Improve Your Support

Peer comments will help you see how you might improve your support. Also, highlight the examples you use to support your point, and ask: Are there any examples that do not really help make the point? What explanations or examples could I add to make my writing clearer or more convincing?

To practice answering these questions, read what a seller posted on craigslist.com about her iPod:

> The silver iPod Mini I am selling is great. I need an iPod with more memory, but this one has nothing wrong with it. I got it for Christmas, and it was a great gift. It is lightweight and in good

condition because it is fairly new. It holds a charge for a long time and can hold a lot of iTunes. It comes with the original case. The price is negotiable. You will want to pursue this great deal! Contact me for more details.

PRACTICE 1

Working with another student or students, answer the following questions.

1. What is the seller's main point?

2. Underline the one sentence that has nothing to do with the main point.

3. Circle any words that do not provide enough information. List three of these terms, and say what details would be useful.

4. What vague word does the author repeat too often?

5. Rewrite the seller's main point/topic sentence to make it more convincing.

PRACTICE 2

Read the two paragraphs that follow, and underline the sentence that does not relate to the main point.

1. Service learning[1] provides excellent opportunities for college students. While students are helping others, they are learning themselves. For example, a student in the medical field who works at a local free clinic provides much-needed assistance, but he is also learning practical skills that relate to his major. He learns about dealing with people who are afraid, who do not know the language, or who are in pain. He might meet someone he likes. When he has to write about his experience for class, he has something real and important to write about. And for many students, working for an organization provides a strong sense of community and purpose. Students have as much to gain from service learning as the organizations they work for do.

[1]service learning: education that combines course work and community service

2. Before choosing roommates, think about your own habits so that you find people whom you can stand living with. For example, if you regularly stay up until 1:00 a.m., you probably should not get a roommate who wants quiet at 10:00 p.m. If you are sloppy and like it that way, do not live with people who demand that you wash every dish every day or clean up after yourself every morning. Cleaning is one of those chores that most people hate. If you want to share all expenses, think about how you will handle discussions on how money should be spent. How much do you want to spend every month, and on what kinds of things do you want to spend it? Roommates can be a blessing for many reasons but only if you can live with them.

PRACTICE 3

To each of the five sentences, add two sentences that give more details.

> **EXAMPLE:** Modern life is full of distractions.
>
> *E-mails and text messages demand our attention.*
>
> *Even bathrooms and grocery carts have advertising.*

1. _____ (your favorite music group) creates music that has an important message.

2. _____ (your favorite sport) is the most exciting sport.

3. Every family has unique traditions that they carry on from one generation to the next.

4. Fast-food restaurants are not completely unhealthy.

5. One person's junk is another person's treasure.

Check the Arrangement of Your Ideas

After you have improved your support by cutting sentences that do not relate to your main idea and adding more details and examples, check that you have ordered and linked your ideas in a way that readers will understand. This process is called improving your writing's **coherence**.

There are three common ways to organize ideas—by time order, space order, and order of importance. Each of these arrangements uses words that help readers move smoothly from one idea to the next. These words are called **transitions**.

Time Order

Use **time order** to present events according to when they happened, as in the following paragraph. Time order is useful for telling stories.

Read the following paragraph, paying attention to the order of ideas and words that link one idea to the next.

> A few months ago, when I was waiting for a train in a subway station, I witnessed a flash mob demonstration. First, I noticed that the station was filling up with more people than usual for a Sunday afternoon. As people kept coming down the stairs, I began to get nervous. Then, someone yelled, "Huh!" and about twenty people yelled back, "Hah!" The yelling was so loud that it echoed down the subway tunnel. During this time, I was just wishing that my train would arrive. But what happened next surprised me. After one person turned on a portable CD player, a bunch of people started dancing as if they were on a stage. Before I knew it, I was part of a large audience that encircled the dancers. As I watched the performance, I was amazed at how well rehearsed it seemed. When it ended, someone went around with a hat, collecting money. I gave a dollar, and I later decided that it was the best entertainment I had ever gotten for such a low price.

The paragraph describes the order of events in the flash mob, moving from the writer's sense of confusion to the performance to the writer's later reflection about the event. Time transitions move the reader from one event to the next.

Time Transitions

after	finally	next	soon
as	first	now	then
before	last	second	when
during	later	since	while

. . . .

PRACTICE 4

In each item in this practice, the first sentence begins a paragraph. Put the rest of the sentences in the paragraph in time order, using **1** for the first event, **2** for the second event, and so on.

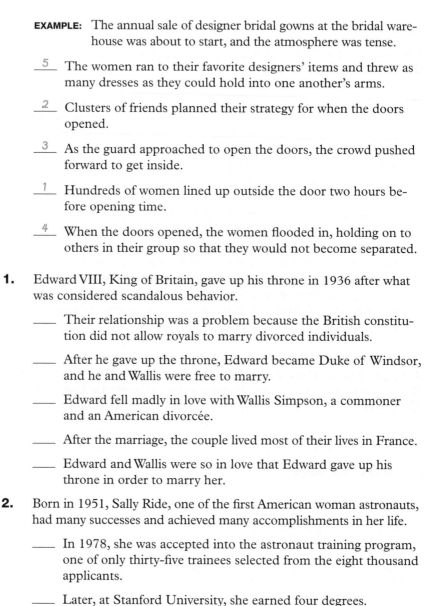

> **EXAMPLE:** The annual sale of designer bridal gowns at the bridal ware-house was about to start, and the atmosphere was tense.
>
> _5_ The women ran to their favorite designers' items and threw as many dresses as they could hold into one another's arms.
>
> _2_ Clusters of friends planned their strategy for when the doors opened.
>
> _3_ As the guard approached to open the doors, the crowd pushed forward to get inside.
>
> _1_ Hundreds of women lined up outside the door two hours before opening time.
>
> _4_ When the doors opened, the women flooded in, holding on to others in their group so that they would not become separated.

1. Edward VIII, King of Britain, gave up his throne in 1936 after what was considered scandalous behavior.

____ Their relationship was a problem because the British constitution did not allow royals to marry divorced individuals.

____ After he gave up the throne, Edward became Duke of Windsor, and he and Wallis were free to marry.

____ Edward fell madly in love with Wallis Simpson, a commoner and an American divorcée.

____ After the marriage, the couple lived most of their lives in France.

____ Edward and Wallis were so in love that Edward gave up his throne in order to marry her.

2. Born in 1951, Sally Ride, one of the first American woman astronauts, had many successes and achieved many accomplishments in her life.

____ In 1978, she was accepted into the astronaut training program, one of only thirty-five trainees selected from the eight thousand applicants.

____ Later, at Stanford University, she earned four degrees.

____ To become an astronaut, she successfully completed a regimen of difficult physical training.

_____ In her youth, she was a star junior tennis player.

_____ In 1983, she became the first American woman to orbit Earth.

Space Order

Use **space order** to present details in a description of a person, place, or thing.

Read the following paragraph, paying attention to the order of ideas and words that link one idea to the next.

> Thirteenth Lake in the Adirondacks of New York is an unspoiled place of beauty. Because the law protects the lake, there are no homes on it, and only nonmotorized boats like canoes and kayaks are allowed. I often just sit at the end of the lake and look out. In front of me, the water is calm and smooth, quietly lapping against the shore. Near the shore, wild brown ducks, a mother leading a line of six or seven ducklings, paddle silently, gliding. Farther out, the water is choppy, forming whitecaps as the wind blows over it. On each side are trees of all sorts, especially huge white birches hanging out over the water. From across the water, loons call to each other, a clear and hauntingly beautiful sound. Beyond the lake are mountains as far as the eye can see, becoming hazier in the distance until they fade out into the horizon. I find peace at Thirteenth Lake, always.

The paragraph describes what the writer sees, starting near and moving farther away. Other ways of using space order are far to near, top to bottom, and side to side. To move readers' attention from one part of the lake to another, the writer uses space transitions.

Space Transitions

above	beyond	next to
across	farther	on the side
at the bottom/top	in front of	over
behind	in the distance	to the left/right/side
below	inside	under
beside	near	

PRACTICE 5

The first sentence of each item below begins a description. Put the phrases that follow it in space order, using **1** for the first detail, **2** for the second detail, and so on. There can be more than one right order for each item. Be ready to explain why you used the order you did.

> **EXAMPLE:** The apartment building I looked at was run-down.
>
> _1_ trash scattered all over the front steps
>
> _3_ boarded-up and broken windows
>
> _4_ tattered plastic bags waving from the roof
>
> _2_ front door swinging open with no lock

1. For once, my blind date was actually good-looking.

_____ muscular arms

_____ flat stomach

_____ long brown hair

_____ dark brown eyes and a nice smile

_____ great legs in tight jeans

2. As the police officer drove toward the accident site, she made note of the scene.

_____ Another police car stopped on the right in the breakdown lane.

_____ Another car was in the middle of the road, its smashed hood smoking.

_____ Two cars spun off to the left, between the northbound and southbound lanes.

_____ Witnesses stood to the right of the police car, speaking to an officer.

Order of Importance

Order of importance builds up to the most important point, putting it last. When you are writing or speaking to convince or persuade someone, order of importance is effective.

Read the following paragraph, paying attention to the order of ideas and words that link one idea to the next.

> The Toyota Prius is definitely the next car that I will buy because it is affordable, safe, and environmentally friendly. I cannot afford a new Prius, but I can buy a used one for somewhere between $10,000 and $13,000. I will need to get a car loan, but it will be a good investment. Using less gas will save me a lot of money in the long run. More important than the price and savings is the safety record of the Prius, which is good. *Consumer Reports* rates the car as safe. Most important to me, however, is that it is a "green" car, making it better for the environment than a regular car. It runs on a combination of electric power and gasoline, which means that it gets higher gas mileage than cars with standard gasoline engines. On the highway, the 2006 Prius gets fifty-one miles per gallon, and in the city the mileage is about forty-four miles per gallon. Because I believe that overuse of gasoline is harmful to the environment, I want to drive a car that does the least harm.

The paragraph states the writer's reasons for wanting to buy a Prius. He ordered the reasons according to how important they are to him, starting with the least important and ending with the most important. Transitions signal the importance of his ideas.

Importance Transitions

above all	more important	most
best	most important	one reason/another reason
especially	another important	worst

PRACTICE 6

The first sentence of each item below begins a paragraph. Put the sentences that follow it in order of importance, using **1** for the first detail, **2** for the second detail, and so on. There can be more than one right order for each item, although the most important detail should be last. Be ready to explain why you used the order you did.

EXAMPLE: Making friends at college is important for several reasons.

   _2_   If you have to miss a class, a friend can help by updating you on lessons and assignments.

<u> 4 </u> Beyond practical concerns, a friend can make you feel a part of the college community and enrich your life.

<u> 3 </u> With a friend, you can study together and quiz each other.

<u> 1 </u> A friend gives you someone to sit with and talk to.

1. I have always wanted to be a police officer.

_____ I understand the risk involved with being a police officer, but at least the job is never boring.

_____ My father was a police officer until he retired four years ago.

_____ I will be able to earn extra money by working overtime on construction projects, security details, and other jobs.

_____ The benefits and job security are good.

2. Laughter is one of life's greatest pleasures.

_____ People who laugh regularly are able to cope better with life's inevitable rough patches.

_____ We tend to be close to people who share a similar sense of humor, so laughter can help us bond with and stay in close touch with friends and family.

_____ Laughter reduces built-up mental stress and gives us a chance to relax.

_____ Laughter helps us to not take ourselves so seriously and "not sweat the small stuff."

Even if you are not using time, space, or importance orders, use transitions to link your ideas. The following are some other ways to use transitions:

PURPOSE	TRANSITIONS
To give an example	for example, for instance, for one thing/for another, one reason/another reason
To add information	also; and; another; in addition; second, third, and so on
To show contrast	although, but, however, in contrast, instead, yet
To indicate a result	as a result, because, so, therefore

Title Your Paragraph

Choose a title for your paragraph that tells the reader what the topic is. Here are some guidelines for choosing a good title:

- It gives the reader an idea of the topic of the paragraph.
- It is usually not a complete sentence.
- It is short and related to your main point.

PRACTICE 7

Either by yourself or with a partner, reread student Patti Terwiller's revised draft on page 42. Then, write two possible titles for it.

PRACTICE 8

Write two possible titles for your draft paragraph.

Check for the Four Basics of a Good Paragraph

When you revise your draft, check that it has these basic features.

Four Basics of a Good Paragraph

1 It has a topic sentence that includes the main point you want to make.

2 It has detailed examples (support) that show, explain, or prove your main point.

3 It is organized logically, and the ideas are joined together with transitions so that readers can move smoothly from one idea to the next.

4 It has a concluding sentence that reminds readers of your main point and makes a statement about it.

Read student Patti Terwiller's draft paragraph below, which you first saw in Chapter 3. Then, read the revised draft with her changes. The colors in the revised paragraph, matched to the Four Basics of a Good Paragraph, show

how Patti used the basics to revise. Notice that most of Patti's changes involved adding detailed examples. She also added transitions, especially time transitions, since her paragraph is organized by time order. She also crossed out words or phrases she did not like.

PATTI'S FIRST DRAFT

> One evening in May, I finally learned to practice self-respect in my relationships. I had always put up with anything my boyfriend did because I was afraid that he might leave me. He was always late and drunk, but I never said anything. He never had any money, and around his friends he either ignored me or was totally rude. At a party, he was ignoring me, as usual, but then something happened. Right in front of me, he was hitting on another girl. Something inside me snapped, and I knew I did not need this. I went up to him, told him our relationship was over, and walked out. He was screaming, but I did not look back. I have not answered his calls; he is history. I have learned about self-respect.

PATTI'S REVISED DRAFT

1 One hot, steamy evening in May, I **3** finally learned to practice self-respect in my relationships. **2** I had always put up with anything my boyfriend did because I was afraid that he might leave me. He was always late and drunk, and he was often abusive, but I never said anything. He never had any money, and around his friends he either ignored me or was totally rude, calling me disrespectful names and cursing at me. At a party **3** in May, he was ignoring me, as usual, ~~but then something happened.~~ **3** Then, right in front of me, he ~~was hitting on~~ started kissing another girl. **3** Next, they were all over each other. **3** And then, my boyfriend smirked right at me. Something inside me snapped, ~~and I knew I did not need this~~. I felt my blood rush to my face. I gritted my teeth for a moment, thinking and gathering my resolve. **3** Then, I narrowed my eyes, ~~went~~ walked up to him, and hissed, "It's over." As I ~~walked~~ stormed out, he was screaming to me, but I did not look back. **3** Since that night, I have not answered his calls or believed his sweet-talking messages, ~~he is history~~. I have learned ~~about self-respect~~ that I do not need him or anyone like him who does not treat me right. **4** What I do need is self-respect, and **3** now I have it.

PRACTICE 9

With a partner, read the first and revised drafts aloud. Talk about why the revised draft is better, and be specific. For example, do not just say, "It has more examples." Discuss why the examples make Patti's experience come alive. Then, answer the following questions.

1. What emotions was Patti feeling? What words showing those emotions are in the revised draft but not in the first draft?

2. What sentence describes what her boyfriend did to anger her the most?

3. What two sentences do you think have the most emotion?

PRACTICE 10

Revise your own draft, thinking about how Patti made her paragraph stronger. Take a close look at your topic and concluding sentences, revising them at least once more. Use the checklist below as a guide.

CHECKLIST

Revising your writing

- ☐ My paragraph fulfills the assignment, and it is written in the appropriate style for the audience and purpose. (Most college assignments should be written in formal English.)
- ☐ My topic sentence is focused on a single topic, is narrow enough for a paragraph, is more than just a simple fact, and is confident (without *I think* or *I hope*).
- ☐ The body sentences have detailed examples that show, explain, or prove my main point.
- ☐ The sentences are organized logically, and transitions link my ideas together.
- ☐ My concluding sentence reminds readers of my main point and ends the paragraph on a strong note.
- ☐ This paragraph is the best I can do, and I am ready to turn it in for a grade.

After you revise your paragraph, you are ready to edit it. When you edit, you read your writing not for ideas (as you do when revising) but for correctness of grammar, punctuation, spelling, and word choice. Chapters 9 through 15 contain information that will help you edit your writing.

PRACTICE 11

Write a letter to your teacher about the paper that you have just revised. You might use the following format:

- Start with the title of your paragraph, and tell your teacher what your main point is.
- Explain why you chose this topic.
- Say what step of the writing process was most difficult and, if you can, explain why.
- State what you think are two strengths of the paragraph (such as a particular detail, sentence, or point), and explain why.
- Tell your teacher what you learned in writing this paragraph and how what you learned might help you write other papers.

5

Developing Your Paragraph

Different Ways to Present Your Ideas

In this course and other college classes, instructors will expect you to express your ideas in logical patterns so that what you say or write is clear. There are nine common patterns: narration, illustration, description, process analysis, classification, definition, comparison and contrast, cause and effect, and argument.

Narration

Narration is telling a story of an event or experience and showing why it is important through details about the experience.

Four Basics of Narration

1 It has a message you want to share with readers (your main point).

2 It includes all the major events of the story (support).

3 It gives details about the major events, bringing the event or experience to life for your readers.

4 It presents the events using time order (according to when things happened).

The numbers and colors in the following paragraph correspond to the Four Basics of Narration.

> **1** In 1848, Ellen and William Craft planned and carried out what I think was a daring escape from the plantation in Georgia

✓ LearningCurve **For extra practice in the skills covered in this chapter, visit**
bedfordstmartins.com/rsinteractive.

where they lived. **2** Ellen and William were both born into slavery before the Civil War. **3** They knew they would never be free while living on their master's plantation. A slave with dark skin, like William, would easily be caught if he tried to go to a northern state. A woman, even if she had light skin like Ellen did, would raise suspicion if she dared to travel on her own. **2** Several years after they got married, Ellen and William came up with an escape plan. **3** They agreed it was risky, but they could no longer face their lives as slaves. **2** First, they would need to save up some money. **3** When he was not working for the master on the plantation, William worked odd jobs in town to earn the cash they required. **2** Next, they used the money to buy a disguise for Ellen. **3** Ellen cut her hair short and wore a suit, glasses, and a top hat. She looked like a white gentleman, and William posed as her servant. **2** Now the Crafts were ready to begin their journey north. **3** Rather than traveling at night and staying hidden, the couple traveled openly by train and steamship. Nobody questioned the right of a white man to travel with his black slave. **2** Ellen and William Craft finally arrived in Philadelphia on Christmas Day in 1848 and lived the rest of their lives in freedom.

1.   Underline the **topic sentence**.

2.   What is important about this event?

3.   What detail made the biggest impression on you? Why?

4.   Circle the **transitions**.

5.   Name one way that the paragraph could be better.

Guided Practice: Narration

By filling in the blanks as indicated, you are applying the Four Basics of Narration in a paragraph. There are no right or wrong answers, so be as creative as you like, and make the paragraph as vivid and interesting as you can. Use your imagination.

TOPIC SENTENCE: Chris and Eva did not believe that their new home was haunted until they moved in and strange things began to happen. **FIRST EVENT:** On their first night in the house, a low moaning kept them awake all night. **DETAILS ABOUT THE MOANING:** _____

_____

_____. **SECOND EVENT:** Then, on the second night, Eva saw a shadowy form behind her as she brushed her teeth. **DETAILS ABOUT THE FORM THAT EVA SAW AND HOW SHE REACTED:** _____

_____

_____

_____. **THIRD EVENT:** On the third night, _____

_____

DETAILS ABOUT THE THIRD EVENT: _____

_____

_____

CONCLUDING SENTENCE: By the end of the week, _____

_____

_____ .

Guided Outline: Narration

Fill in the outline with events and details that support the topic sentence. Try prewriting to get ideas, and arrange the events according to time order.

TOPIC SENTENCE: The _____ (funniest / saddest / most emotional / most embarrassing / scariest) thing that I ever _____ (saw / experienced) was _____ .

FIRST EVENT: _____

    DETAILS: _____

SECOND EVENT: _____

    DETAILS: _____

THIRD EVENT: _____

    DETAILS: _____

CONCLUDING SENTENCE: Whenever I remember that time, I think _____

_____

_____ .

TIP To complete this chapter, you will need to know about prewriting (Chapter 2); writing the main point (topic sentence), supporting that point, and planning/ outlining (Chapter 3); and using transitions and revising (Chapter 4).

Write a Narration Paragraph

Write a narration paragraph using the outline that you developed or a topic of your own. Then, complete the narration checklist below.

CHECKLIST

Evaluating your narration paragraph

- ☐ My writing style is appropriate for the audience and purpose. (Most college assignments should be written in formal English.)
- ☐ My topic sentence states what is important about the event or experience.
- ☐ I have included all the important events with details so that readers can understand what happened.
- ☐ The paragraph has *all* the Four Basics of Narration (p. 45).
- ☐ I have included transitions to move readers smoothly from one event to the next.
- ☐ I have reread the paragraph, making at least three improvements and checking for grammar and spelling errors.

Illustration

Illustration uses examples to show, explain, or prove a point.

Four Basics of Illustration

1 It has a main point to illustrate.

2 It gives specific examples to show, explain, or prove the point.

3 It gives details to support the examples.

4 It uses enough examples to get the point across.

The numbers and colors in the following paragraph correspond to the Four Basics of Illustration.

4
Enough examples to make the writer's point

> **1** Although people starting out in the nursing field may feel that they do not have any relevant work experience, they may actually have gained valuable and transferrable skills in other jobs, which they may possibly have held earlier. **2** For example, working in a restaurant does not sound as though it would be a job that

Illustration　49

would particularly help a person prepare for a career in nursing, but, in fact, it can. **3** Like nursing, restaurant work requires good listening skills, a sharp memory, and constant attention to detail. It builds experience in dealing with demanding customers who might not always be at their best. And working in a restaurant can also help a person develop the important skills of prioritizing and multitasking. **2** Caring for young children is another job that can provide some relevant background experience to a person who is entering the nursing profession. **3** Child-care workers as well as parents develop important communication skills, patience, and compassion that can be helpful if they enter a career in nursing. The steady and capable caregiving skills gained from work with children can help prepare nursing students for caring for others, of any age. **2** A third type of background, customer service, can also establish a groundwork of relevant experience for beginning nursing students. **3** A demanding job as a retail salesclerk, receptionist, cashier, or landscape worker requires the ability to do hard jobs, keep focused, and interact with many different kinds of people. **1** All of these skills—multitasking, caregiving, listening and communicating well, relating to people—are essential to being a good nurse, and they can all be learned in a variety of jobs.

4 Enough examples to make the writer's point

1. Underline the **topic sentence**.
2. In your own words, what is the point the writer wants to make?
3. Circle the **transitions**.
4. What is another example the writer might give?

Guided Practice: Illustration

The paragraph that follows is an illustration, and by filling in the blanks as indicated, you will be applying the Four Basics of Illustration in a paragraph. There are no right or wrong answers. What is important is writing good examples and details about them.

TOPIC SENTENCE: Most people know which of their habits are bad ones, but that does not mean that they can break those bad habits.

FIRST EXAMPLE: One common bad habit is _____.

DETAILS ABOUT FIRST BAD HABIT: Not only is _____
_____ bad, it is also _____
_____ . **SECOND EXAMPLE:** Another bad
habit is eating junk food. **DETAILS ABOUT SECOND EXAMPLE:** _____
_____
_____
_____. **THIRD EXAMPLE:** One of the worst bad
habits that people have is _____.
DETAILS ABOUT THIRD EXAMPLE: _____
_____
_____
_____. **CONCLUDING SENTENCE:** Of course, I _____
_____
_____
_____ .

Guided Outline: Illustration

Fill in the outline with examples and details that support the topic sentence. Try prewriting to get ideas.

TOPIC SENTENCE: Today's college students have many _____
_____ (choices /stresses /roles . . .).

FIRST EXAMPLE: _____

    DETAILS: _____

SECOND EXAMPLE: _____

    DETAILS: _____

THIRD EXAMPLE: _____

    DETAILS: _____

CONCLUDING SENTENCE: Going to college is not easy, (and /but /so) ___
_____
_____
_____ .

Write an Illustration Paragraph

Write an illustration paragraph using the outline you developed or a topic of your own. Then, complete the illustration checklist below.

CHECKLIST

Evaluating your illustration paragraph

☐ My writing style is appropriate for the audience and purpose. (Most college assignments should be written in formal English.)

☐ My topic sentence states my main point, is more than just a simple fact, and is confident (without *I think* or *I hope*).

☐ I have included several detailed examples that will help readers understand my point.

☐ The paragraph has *all* the Four Basics of Illustration (p. 48).

☐ I have included transitions to move readers smoothly from one example to the next.

☐ I have reread the paragraph, making improvements and checking for grammar and spelling errors.

Description

Description creates a strong impression of your topic: It shows how the topic looks, sounds, smells, tastes, or feels.

Four Basics of Description

1 It creates a main impression — an overall effect or image — about the topic.

2 It uses specific examples to create the impression.

3 It supports the examples with details that appeal to the senses — sight, hearing, smell, taste, and touch.

4 It brings a person, a place, or an object to life for the readers.

The numbers and colors in the following paragraph correspond to the Four Basics of Description.

1 Late at night, the ocean near my grandmother's house always fills me with wonder. **2** It is dark, lit only by the moon. **3** When the moon is full, the light reflects off the water, bouncing up and

4 Examples and details bring the subject to life.

shining on the waves as they start to break. When the clouds cover the moon, the darkness is complete. The world stands still and silent for a moment. **2** Then, I hear the waves **3** coming toward me, swelling, breaking, and bursting into surf that I cannot see. I hear them gently go back, only to start again. **2** Gulls call in the distance. **3** During the day, their call sounds raw, but at night it softens and sounds like a plea. **2** Now that I am in touch with my senses, I am hit with a smell of salt and dampness that **3** seems to coat my lungs. **2** I stand completely still, just experiencing the beach, as if I have become a part of the elements. The experience always calms me and takes away the strains of everyday life.

4
Examples and details bring the subject to life.

1.   What impression does the writer want to create?

2.   Underline the **topic sentence**.

3.   Double-underline the **example** that makes the strongest impression on you. Why did you choose this example?

4.   Add another sensory detail to one of the examples.

5.   Try rewriting the topic sentence.

Guided Practice: Description

By filling in the blanks as indicated, you are applying the Four Basics of Description in a paragraph. There are no right or wrong answers. What is important is creating a strong impression on your reader by using vivid details. Use your imagination.

TOPIC SENTENCE: The apartment that I saw this morning was so _____ _____ that I _____ _____. FIRST EXAMPLE TO CREATE THE IMPRESSION: As soon as we opened the front door, _____ _____. DESCRIPTIVE DETAIL ABOUT FIRST EXAMPLE: _____ _____. SECOND EXAMPLE TO CREATE THE IMPRESSION: _____. DESCRIPTIVE DETAIL: _____. THIRD EXAMPLE: _____

DESCRIPTIVE DETAIL: _____.

DESCRIPTIVE DETAIL: _____.

CONCLUDING SENTENCE: After seeing this apartment, I _____

_____.

Guided Outline: Description

Fill in the outline with examples and details that support the topic sentence. Try prewriting to get ideas.

       TOPIC SENTENCE: The _____ on this campus is _____.

       FIRST EXAMPLE: _____

          DETAILS: _____

       SECOND EXAMPLE: _____

          DETAILS: _____

       THIRD EXAMPLE: _____

          DETAILS: _____

       CONCLUDING SENTENCE: Every time I am there, I think _____

_____.

Write a Description Paragraph

Write a description paragraph, using the outline you developed or a topic of your own. Then, complete the description checklist below.

CHECKLIST

Evaluating your description paragraph

☐ My writing style is appropriate for the audience and purpose. (Most college assignments should be written in formal English.)

☐ My topic sentence includes the main impression that I want to create for readers.

☐ I include examples that show the readers what I mean.

☐ The paragraph has _all_ the Four Basics of Description (p. 51).

☐ I have included transitions to move readers smoothly from one example to the next.

☐ I have reread the paragraph, making improvements and checking for grammar and spelling errors.

Process Analysis

Process analysis either explains how to do something (so that readers can do it) or how something works (so that readers understand it).

Four Basics of Process Analysis

1 It tells readers either how to do the steps of the process or how something works.

2 It includes the major steps in the process.

3 It explains each step in detail.

4 It presents the steps in the order they happen (time order).

The numbers and colors in the following paragraph correspond to the Four Basics of Process Analysis.

1
Readers told how to do something

4
Steps presented in the order they need to happen.

People always ask for the recipe for the simplest cookie that I make, and I am always a little embarrassed to give it to them. **1** Here is how to make delicious cookies with almost no effort. **2** First, buy two ingredients—a roll of sugar-cookie dough from your supermarket's refrigerated section and a bag of mini peanut butter cups. Cut the roll into half-inch slices, and then cut each slice in half. Next, roll the pieces into balls. Then, grease a mini-muffin pan and put the balls in the pan. Start baking the dough according to the directions on the sugar-cookie package. When the cookies are about three minutes from being done, take them out. Press a peanut butter cup into the center of each ball, and return the cookies to the oven until they are golden brown. When they are cool, pop them out of the muffin pans. These cookies are so easy to make that even little children can help. Enjoy!

1. Underline the **topic sentence**.

2. How many steps does the writer describe?

3. Could you perform the process after reading the paragraph? If not, where do you need more information?

4. Circle the **transitions**.

5. Which of the Four Basics does this paragraph lack? Revise the paragraph so that it includes this basic.

Guided Practice: Process Analysis

By filling in the blanks as indicated, you are applying the Four Basics of Process Analysis in a paragraph. There are no right or wrong answers. What is important is including all the key steps and explaining them.

TOPIC SENTENCE: In order to protect your skin from sun damage, it is important to take the following precautions. **FIRST STEP IN PROCESS:** First, _____

_____.

EXPLANATION OF FIRST STEP: _____

_____. **SECOND STEP:** _____

_____.

EXPLANATION OF SECOND STEP: _____

_____.

THIRD STEP: _____.

EXPLANATION OF THIRD STEP: _____

_____.

(Add other steps and explanations.) **LAST STEP:** Finally, _____

_____.

CONCLUDING SENTENCE: Without being careful, _____

_____.

Guided Outline: Process Analysis

Fill in the outline with the steps in the process and detailed explanations of them. Try prewriting to get ideas, and organize the steps according to time order.

TOPIC SENTENCE: Learning how to _____

(something you do well) is not hard if you _____

_____.

FIRST STEP: _____

    EXPLANATION: _____

SECOND STEP: _____

    EXPLANATION: _____

THIRD STEP: _____

    EXPLANATION: _____

CONCLUDING SENTENCE: _____ takes some

practice and concentration, but anyone can do it.

Write a Process Analysis Paragraph

Write a process analysis paragraph, using the outline that you developed or a topic of your own. Then, complete the process analysis checklist below.

CHECKLIST

Evaluating your process analysis paragraph

☐ My writing style is appropriate for the audience and purpose. (Most college assignments should be written in formal English.)

☐ My topic sentence tells readers what process I am writing about in this paragraph, and it is confident (without *I think* or *I hope*).

☐ I have included all the major steps and details about them.

☐ The paragraph has *all* the Four Basics of Process Analysis (p. 54).

☐ I have included transitions to move readers smoothly from one step to the next.

☐ I have reread the paragraph, making improvements and checking for grammar and spelling errors.

Classification

Classification sorts people or things into categories so that they can be understood.

Four Basics of Classification

1 It makes sense of a group of people or things by sorting them into useful categories.

2 It has a purpose for sorting.

3 It includes categories that follow a single organizing principle (for example, to sort by size, by color, by price, and so on).

4 It gives detailed examples or explanations of things that fit into each category.

The numbers and colors in the following paragraph correspond to the Four Basics of Classification.

1 Over the past several years, three kinds of diets have been **2** very popular in this country. **3** The first one was the low-fat diet. **4** Dieters had to limit their fat intake, so they stayed away from foods like nuts, fatty meats, ice cream, and fried foods. They could eat lots of low-fat foods like pasta, bread, fruits, and vegetables, as well as lean meat, fish, and chicken. **3** The second kind of diet was the low-carbohydrate plan. **4** The first popular low-carb diet was the Atkins plan. Under this plan, dieters could eat all the fatty meats, butter, cheese, and nuts they wanted. Some people were eating a whole pound of bacon for breakfast with eggs and butter. However, they could not eat bread, pasta, or most fruits. On this plan, people lost a lot of weight quickly, but many found that they could not stick with a diet that did not allow carbs. The South Beach diet was also a low-carb plan, but not quite as strict as the Atkins diet, at least after the first two weeks. **3** The third diet plan, one that has been around for a long time, is Weight Watchers. **4** It requires that dieters eat smaller portions of most foods—everything in moderation. Points are assigned to foods, and dieters must stay within a certain number of points each day. High-calorie foods have a high number of points, and many vegetables have no points. Americans have spent millions on these diet plans, but the obesity rate continues to increase. It seems that the "right" kind of diet, one that allows people to lose weight and keep it off, has yet to be invented.

1. Underline the **topic sentence**.
2. What are the categories?
3. Circle the **transitions**.
4. What is the purpose of the classification?
5. What is the organizing principle?
6. Try rewriting the concluding sentence in your own words.

Guided Practice: Classification

By filling in the blanks as indicated, you are applying the Four Basics of Classification in a paragraph. There are no right or wrong answers. What is important is stating the categories and giving examples of what fits into them.

TOPIC SENTENCE: If I had enough money, I would own _____ homes in different locations so that I could always go where I wanted and do my favorite things. **FIRST CATEGORY:** First, I would want a home located _____. **EXPLANATION:** Here I would pass the time by _____ and _____. **SECOND CATEGORY:** Second, I would want a home located _____ _____. **EXPLANATION:** This home would be my place to _____ and _____ anytime I wanted. **(ADD MORE CATEGORIES AND EXPLANATIONS IF NEEDED)** **LAST CATEGORY:** Finally, my most treasured home would be located _____. **EXPLANATION:** This home would be my favorite because _____. **CONCLUDING SENTENCE:** Although _____, I still like to dream about _____ because _____.

Guided Outline: Classification

Fill in the outline with the categories and detailed examples or explanations of what fits into them. Try prewriting to get ideas.

TOPIC SENTENCE: Like most people, I have several different kinds of _____ (collections / clothes / coworkers / moods . . .).

FIRST CATEGORY: _____

    EXAMPLE/EXPLANATION OF WHAT FITS INTO THE CATEGORY: _____

    _____

    _____

SECOND CATEGORY: _____

    EXAMPLE/EXPLANATION OF WHAT FITS INTO THE CATEGORY: _____

    _____

    _____

THIRD CATEGORY: _____

    EXAMPLE/EXPLANATION OF WHAT FITS INTO THE CATEGORY: _____

    _____

    _____

    _____

CONCLUDING SENTENCE: Even though my _____ are

different, they are all _____ to me.

Write a Classification Paragraph

Write a classification paragraph, using the outline that you developed or a topic of your own. Then, complete the classification checklist below.

CHECKLIST
Evaluating your classification paragraph
☐ My writing style is appropriate for the audience and purpose. (Most college assignments should be written in formal English.)
☐ My topic sentence tells readers what I am classifying.
☐ I have stated the categories and given examples of what is in them.
☐ The paragraph has *all* the Four Basics of Classification (p. 56).
☐ Transitions move readers smoothly from one category to the next.
☐ I have reread the paragraph, making improvements and checking for grammar and spelling errors.

Definition

Definition explains what a term or concept means.

Four Basics of Definition

1 It tells readers what is being defined.

2 It gives a clear definition.

3 It gives examples to explain the definition.

4 It gives details about the examples that readers will understand.

The numbers and colors in the following paragraph correspond to the Four Basics of Definition.

> **1** Propaganda **2** is information that is promoted to support certain views or messages. It can come in many forms, but its purpose is to persuade us to see things a certain way. **3** For example, the president of the United States may give televised speeches to convince us that some policy or action he supports is right. **4** We may get mailings on the subject. People who agree with the president's message may speak in favor of it on talk shows or in interviews. **3** Religious organizations may spread propaganda about the importance of certain actions (or avoiding certain actions). **4** For example, many churches sent positive messages to their members about the religious importance of the movie *The Chronicles of Narnia*. Churches urged their members to see the movie and even had their own showings, hoping the film would increase church attendance. **3** Propaganda can be good, as when a health organization sends information about how to avoid unhealthy behavior and follow good habits, or bad, as when one political group publishes false or exaggerated information to attack another group. Because we are surrounded by propaganda, it is important that we think about who is behind the message and whether we believe the information.

1.   Underline the **topic sentence**.

2.   What is the term being defined?

3.   In your own words, what does the term mean?

4.   Give another example that would help define the term.

5.   Add a **transition** that would be useful.

Guided Practice: Definition

By filling in the blanks as indicated, you are applying the Four Basics of Definition in a paragraph. There are no right or wrong answers. What is important is stating the meaning of the word and giving examples that will help your reader to understand it as you do. As you fill in the blanks, think of someone that you believe is a hero.

TOPIC SENTENCE: A *hero* is someone who _____

_____. **FIRST**

EXAMPLE: A hero cares about what happens to others. **DETAIL ABOUT**

FIRST EXAMPLE: For example, _____

_____.

SECOND EXAMPLE: A hero also is not afraid to _____

_____. **DETAIL:** If a hero _____

_____, he or she will _____

_____. **THIRD EXAMPLE:** A hero also _____

_____. **DETAIL:** _____

_____. **CONCLUDING**

SENTENCE: A hero is _____, and

I _____.

Guided Outline: Definition

Fill in the outline with a definition and examples and details that explain the definition. Try prewriting to get ideas.

TOPIC SENTENCE: A *family* is a group of people who _____.

FIRST EXAMPLE: _____

    DETAILS: _____

SECOND EXAMPLE: _____

    DETAILS: _____

THIRD EXAMPLE: _____

    DETAILS: _____

CONCLUDING SENTENCE: Families are _____

_____

_____

_____.

(Do not repeat the definition from your topic sentence.)

Write a Definition Paragraph

Write a definition paragraph, using the outline you developed or a topic of your own. Then, complete the definition checklist below.

CHECKLIST

Evaluating your definition paragraph

☐ My writing style is appropriate for the audience and purpose. (Most college assignments should be written in formal English.)

☐ My topic sentence tells readers what I am defining and gives a basic definition.

☐ I have given examples and details that show readers what the term means as I am defining it.

☐ The paragraph has *all* the Four Basics of Definition (p. 59).

☐ I have included transitions to move readers smoothly from one example to the next.

☐ I have reread the paragraph, making improvements and checking for grammar and spelling errors.

Comparison and Contrast

Comparison shows the similarities among people, ideas, situations, and things; **contrast** shows the differences.

Four Basics of Comparison and Contrast

1 It has subjects (usually two) that are enough alike to be usefully compared or contrasted.

2 It serves a purpose — to help readers either make a decision about two subjects or understand them.

3 It gives several points of comparison and/or contrast.

4 It uses one of two organizations — **point-by-point** or **whole-to-whole**.

POINT-BY-POINT	WHOLE-TO-WHOLE

1. First point of comparison
    Subject 1
    Subject 2
	1. Subject 1
	    First point of comparison
	    Second point of comparison
	    Third point of comparison

POINT-BY-POINT	WHOLE-TO-WHOLE

2. Second point of comparison
    Subject 1
    Subject 2
3. Third point of comparison
    Subject 1
    Subject 2
	2. Subject 2
	    First point of comparison
	    Second point of comparison
	    Third point of comparison

The numbers and colors in the following paragraph correspond to the Four Basics of Comparison and Contrast.

1 Greenline Bank **2** suits my needs much better than **1** Worldly Bank does. **3** For one thing, there are not any hidden charges at Greenline. For example, customers get free checking even if they keep a low balance in their accounts. Since I do not usually have much in my checking account, this is important for me. In contrast, to get free checking at Worldly Bank, customers must have a minimum balance of $3,000. That would mean that I pay for every check I write, and I do not need that charge. **3** Another way that Greenline Bank is better is that it offers low interest rates on loans. If I need a loan for something like a new car, for example, the bank's rate of interest on that would be 9 percent. Worldly Bank would charge 17.5 percent for the same loan. Over a three-year period, the difference between 9 percent and 17.5 percent is huge. **3** Another difference between the two banks is that Greenline Bank is a small, local bank. People know me when I walk in, and I feel that I can trust them. I also believe that giving Greenline my business helps the local economy in some small way. In contrast, Worldly Bank is huge. The people in the local office are polite in a businesslike way, but I do not feel as if I know them. Worldly Bank as a whole is the fourth-largest bank in the country, so I know that my little account means nothing to it. Because of these differences, I am a loyal Greenline Bank customer.

4 Uses one type of organization throughout.

1. Underline the **topic sentence**.

2. Is the purpose to help readers make a choice or to help them understand?

3. Does the paragraph compare or contrast?

4. What kind of organization does it use?

5. What are the points of comparison?

Guided Practice: Comparison and Contrast

By filling in the blanks as indicated, you are applying the Four Basics of Comparison and Contrast in a paragraph. There are no right or wrong answers. What is important is the points you make to show the differences and the details you give about those differences.

TOPIC SENTENCE: I had no idea how different high school and college would be. **FIRST POINT OF CONTRAST:** One big difference between them is that in high school _____,
while in college _____. **SECOND POINT OF CONTRAST:** Another difference is _____. In high school _____. In contrast, in college _____. **THIRD POINT OF CONTRAST:** One of the most important differences between high school and college is _____. For example, _____, whereas _____. **CONCLUDING SENTENCE:** While high school is _____, college is _____.

Guided Outline: Comparison and Contrast

Fill in the outline with the points of comparison between the two subjects. Try prewriting to get ideas, and save the most important point of comparison for last.

TOPIC SENTENCE: _____ (falling in love / learning to drive / the first week of a new job . . .) can be just like

_____

_____

_____.

SUBJECT 1

    FIRST POINT OF COMPARISON: _____

    SECOND POINT OF COMPARISON: _____

    THIRD POINT OF COMPARISON: _____

SUBJECT 2

    FIRST POINT OF COMPARISON: _____

    SECOND POINT OF COMPARISON: _____

    THIRD POINT OF COMPARISON: _____

CONCLUDING SENTENCE: The important thing about both is that _____

_____

_____

_____ .

Write a Comparison-and-Contrast Paragraph

Write a comparison or contrast paragraph, using the outline you developed or a topic of your own. Then, complete the comparison-and-contrast checklist below.

CHECKLIST

Evaluating your comparison-and-contrast paragraph

☐ My writing style is appropriate for the audience and purpose. (Most college assignments should be written in formal English.)

☐ My topic sentence tells readers what my subjects are and whether I am comparing them, contrasting them, or both.

☐ I have detailed points of comparison or contrast between the two subjects.

☐ The paragraph has *all* the Four Basics of Comparison and Contrast (p. 62).

☐ I have included transitions to move readers smoothly from one point or subject to the next.

☐ I have reread the paragraph, making improvements and checking for grammar and spelling errors.

Cause and Effect

A **cause** is what makes something happen. An **effect** is what happens as a result of something.

A ring diagram is useful to show causes and effects of something.

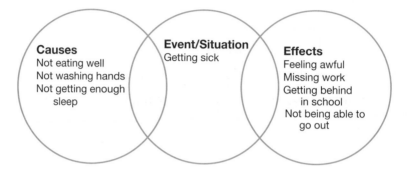

Four Basics of Cause and Effect

1 The main point reflects the writer's purpose — to explain causes, effects, or both.

2 If the purpose is to explain causes, it gives real causes, not just things that happened before. For example, the fact that you ate a hot dog before you got a speeding ticket does not mean that the hot dog caused the ticket.

3 If the purpose is to explain effects, it gives real effects, not just things that happened after. For example, getting a speeding ticket was not the effect of eating the hot dog; it simply happened after you ate the hot dog.

4 It gives readers detailed examples or explanations of the causes and/or effects.

The numbers and colors in the following paragraph correspond to the Four Basics of Cause and Effect.

1 Apple iPods and other portable listening devices may cause hearing loss in several ways, if people are not careful. **2** First, these devices often use earbuds. Earbuds come in many different varieties, and some have built-in microphones for phone calls. **4** Because these snug-fitting headphones deliver the music directly into the ear canal, **3** they can damage the eardrum. **2** Second, people listening to portable devices often turn the volume up to unsafe levels. **4** Some experts say volume levels that are higher than 80 percent of maximum **3** can harm the delicate parts of the inner ear. **2** The third, and perhaps most surprising, way that portable devices cause hearing loss is that people listen to them for too long. Before MP3 players and iPods, portable listening devices could hold only one tape or CD at a time, and hearing loss was rarely a problem. Now, with so many hours of music available on one small device, we can listen for many hours without taking a break. **4** In order to prevent permanent hearing damage, physicians recommend listening for no more than ninety minutes per day. Taking good care of your ears now, by listening at safe volumes for limited periods of time, will allow you to continue enjoying music throughout your life.

1. Underline the **topic sentence**.

2. What is the writer's purpose?

3. What are three causes of iPod hearing loss?

4. What are two effects explained in the paragraph?

5. Circle the sentence that is neither a cause nor an effect of iPod hearing loss.

Guided Practice: Cause and Effect

By filling in the blanks as indicated, you are applying the Four Basics of Cause and Effect in a paragraph. There are no right or wrong answers. What is important is showing, in this case, what caused you not to have your homework. Feel free to be creative with your causes.

TOPIC SENTENCE: I did not do my homework assignment, but after you hear my reason, I hope that you will not mark me down for not having done it. **FIRST CAUSE:** Yesterday morning, _____

_____ . **DETAIL ABOUT FIRST CAUSE:**

Believe it or not, I had to _____

_____ . **SECOND CAUSE:** Later that day,

_____ .

DETAIL: It was so bad that _____

_____ . **THIRD CAUSE:** Then, last night, _____

_____ .

DETAIL: I had to _____ .

EFFECT: As a result of all these things, ⎯⎯⎯⎯⎯⎯⎯⎯⎯⎯

⎯⎯⎯⎯⎯⎯⎯⎯⎯⎯⎯⎯⎯⎯⎯⎯⎯⎯⎯⎯⎯⎯⎯ .

CONCLUDING SENTENCE: I hope you can see ⎯⎯⎯⎯⎯⎯⎯⎯ ,

and ⎯⎯⎯⎯⎯⎯⎯⎯⎯⎯⎯⎯⎯⎯⎯⎯⎯⎯⎯⎯⎯⎯ .

Guided Outline: Cause and Effect

Fill in the outline with the detailed examples or explanations of effects. Try prewriting to get ideas, and save the most important effect for last.

   TOPIC SENTENCE: I never expected so much to happen as a result

of my decision to ⎯⎯⎯⎯⎯⎯⎯⎯⎯⎯⎯⎯⎯⎯⎯⎯⎯⎯ .

   FIRST EFFECT: ⎯⎯⎯⎯⎯⎯⎯⎯⎯⎯⎯⎯⎯⎯⎯⎯⎯⎯⎯⎯

      DETAILS: ⎯⎯⎯⎯⎯⎯⎯⎯⎯⎯⎯⎯⎯⎯⎯⎯⎯⎯⎯⎯

   SECOND EFFECT: ⎯⎯⎯⎯⎯⎯⎯⎯⎯⎯⎯⎯⎯⎯⎯⎯⎯⎯

      DETAILS: ⎯⎯⎯⎯⎯⎯⎯⎯⎯⎯⎯⎯⎯⎯⎯⎯⎯⎯⎯⎯

   THIRD EFFECT: ⎯⎯⎯⎯⎯⎯⎯⎯⎯⎯⎯⎯⎯⎯⎯⎯⎯⎯⎯

      DETAILS: ⎯⎯⎯⎯⎯⎯⎯⎯⎯⎯⎯⎯⎯⎯⎯⎯⎯⎯⎯⎯

   CONCLUDING SENTENCE: All of this reminded me that ⎯⎯⎯⎯⎯⎯

⎯⎯⎯⎯⎯⎯⎯⎯⎯⎯⎯⎯⎯⎯⎯⎯⎯⎯⎯⎯⎯⎯⎯ .

Write a Cause-and-Effect Paragraph

Write a cause-and-effect paragraph, using the outline that you developed or a topic of your own. Then, complete the cause-and-effect checklist below.

CHECKLIST

Evaluating your cause-and-effect paragraph

☐ My writing style is appropriate for the audience and purpose. (Most college assignments should be written in formal English.)

☐ My topic sentence includes my topic and whether I am writing about causes, effects, or both.

☐ I have written details about causes or effects so that my readers will understand them.

☐ The paragraph has *all* the Four Basics of Cause and Effect (p. 66).

☐ I have included transitions to move readers smoothly from one cause or effect to the next.

☐ I have reread the paragraph, making improvements and checking for grammar and spelling errors.

Argument

Argument takes a position on an issue and gives detailed reasons that defend or support it. You use argument to persuade someone to see things your way and / or to take an action. Being able to argue well is important in every area of your life.

Four Basics of Argument

1 It takes a strong and definite position.

2 It gives good reasons and evidence to defend the position.

3 It considers opposing positions.

4 It has enthusiasm and energy from start to finish.

The numbers and colors in the following paragraph correspond to the Four Basics of Argument.

1 Rap singers should change what they talk about. **2** One reason that they should change is that they talk about women in a disrespectful way. Rap singers should stop calling women "hos" and other negative terms. Most women resent being called these terms, and calling women names encourages men to treat them badly. Rap songs also make violence toward women seem manly and reasonable. **2** Another reason to change topics is that the lyrics promote violence, crime, and drugs in general. When young people are shooting each other in cities around the country, something is wrong, and no one should be making it seem glamorous, courageous, or manly. That is what rap lyrics do. **3** Some people say that rap songs are just music, not causes of anything but enjoyment. But I disagree: Many young people listen carefully to rap lyrics and are affected by the words. **2** The most important reason that rap singers should change topics is that they have a chance to make things better rather than glorifying violence. Rap singers could be a strong force for positive change. They could help our cities and our country. Rap singers can sing about whatever they like: Why can't they sing for the good of all?

4 Argument has energy from start to finish.

1. Underline the **topic sentence**.

2. What is the topic?

3. What is the writer's position?

4. What three reasons does the writer give to support the position?

5. Name one detail that the writer could add to make the paragraph stronger.

6. Rewrite the topic sentence to make it stronger.

Guided Practice: Argument

By filling in the blanks as indicated, you are applying the Four Basics of Argument in a paragraph. There are no right or wrong answers. What is important is strongly stating your position on something and supporting it with good reasons.

TOPIC SENTENCE: Recently on this campus, there has been talk of

_____, and I do / do not believe that _____

_____ .

ACKNOWLEDGING OPPOSING POSITION: Some people say that _____

_____ . **FIRST REASON:**

However, I say that _____ .

DETAIL ABOUT FIRST REASON: For example, _____

_____ . **SECOND REASON:**

Another reason I believe / do not believe _____

_____ . **DETAIL:**

It would _____ .

THIRD REASON: The most important reason for / against _____

_____

is that _____

_____ . **DETAIL:** That is good / bad because

_____ .

CONCLUDING SENTENCE: If we do / do not _____ ,

we will _____ .

Guided Outline: Argument

Fill in the outline with reasons, and details about the reasons, that support the position in the topic sentence. Try prewriting to get ideas, and save the most important reason for last.

TOPIC SENTENCE: It should be legal / illegal for the government to listen in on U.S. citizens' phone conversations without having to get a warrant.

FIRST REASON: _____

     DETAILS: _____

SECOND REASON: _____

     DETAILS: _____

THIRD REASON: _____

     DETAILS: _____

CONCLUDING SENTENCE: _____

_____ .

Write an Argument Paragraph

Write an argument paragraph, using the outline that you developed or a topic of your own. Then, complete the argument checklist below.

CHECKLIST

Evaluating your argument paragraph

☐ My writing style is appropriate for the audience and purpose. (Most college assignments should be written in formal English.)

☐ My topic sentence states my topic and a strong position on that topic.

☐ I have given solid reasons, and details about them to support my position.

☐ My paragraph has *all* the Four Basics of Argument (p. 69).

☐ I have included transitions to move readers smoothly from one reason or example to the next.

☐ I have reread the paragraph, making improvements and checking for grammar and spelling errors.

6

Moving from Paragraphs to Essays

How to Write Longer Papers

Essay Structure

An essay has multiple paragraphs and three necessary parts:

ESSAY PART	CONTENTS/PURPOSE OF THE PART
1. An **introduction**	includes a thesis statement that states the main point. The introduction is usually the first paragraph.
2. A **body**	includes at least three paragraphs. Each paragraph usually begins with a topic sentence that supports the thesis statement. Each topic sentence is supported by examples and details in the rest of the paragraph.
3. A **conclusion**	reminds readers of the main point, just as the concluding sentence of a paragraph does. The conclusion in an essay is usually the last paragraph. It summarizes the support and makes an observation.

✓ **LearningCurve** For extra practice in the skills covered in this chapter, visit bedfordstmartins.com/rsinteractive.

The following diagram shows how the parts of an essay relate to the parts of a paragraph.

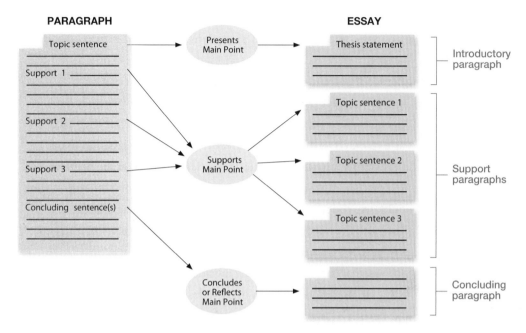

Read the following essay, noticing how the introduction, body, and conclusion paragraphs differ from each other.

> Demand for medical professionals is high, and it is expected to grow over the next decade. Although physicians are always needed, medicine offers many other kinds of jobs that provide satisfaction and good salaries.

Introduction

Thesis statement

> One of the high-demand professions is that of radiology technician. These professionals perform ultrasounds, take X-rays, and do mammograms and magnetic resonance imaging (MRI) tests. Radiology technicians must operate expensive, sensitive machines with great care and accuracy. They must also have good people skills because they will encounter patients who are nervous about tests. The average starting salary for these technicians is $44,000.

> Another high-demand profession is nursing. With the average age of Americans on the rise, many more nurses are needed to supply good health care to the aging population. Registered nurses are in

Body paragraphs

Body paragraphs

short supply all over the United States, and hospitals are competing with one another to hire them. These nurses provide a wide range of patient care, such as documenting symptoms, administering medicines, and working with physicians. Registered nurses' average starting wage is $22 an hour, and many nurses can expect to be offered large bonuses when they agree to accept a position.

The highest demand in the medical field is for pharmacists. Pharmacists dispense drugs prescribed by doctors, but their role has expanded as more people rely on them for information about medications, interactions among medications, and side effects. Pharmacists must be precise and must read carefully; otherwise, they could give the wrong medication or the wrong dosage. Because a shortage of trained pharmacists exists, the average starting salary is over $80,000 and rising.

Conclusion

Medical careers offer many advantages, including the ability to find a job in almost any area of the country as well as good salaries and benefits. Trained radiology technicians, nurses, and pharmacists are likely to remain in high demand as the population ages, as scientists discover new cures, and as technology advances.

Essays can be short or long, depending on the writer's purpose and on the assignment. In this course, you may be asked to write essays that have five paragraphs—an introduction, three body paragraphs, and a conclusion.

Write an Essay

The process of writing an essay is the same process you have used to write a paragraph. The steps in this section will help you write an essay, but if you need more explanations and practices, go back to Chapters 2–4, which have more details about each of the steps.

Get Ideas

(See Chapter 2.)

- Narrow and explore your topic (prewrite).

Write

(See Chapter 3.)

- State your main point (thesis statement).
- Write topic sentences for each major point supporting the thesis statement, and write paragraphs that support each topic sentence.
- Make an outline or plan of your ideas.
- Write a draft.
- Reread your draft, taking notes about what would make it better.

Rewrite

(See Chapter 4.)

- Rewrite your draft, making the changes you noted (and more).
- Reread the new draft, making sure it is as good as you can make it.

Edit

(See Chapters 9–15.)

- Read your paper for grammar, punctuation, and spelling errors.

Narrow Your Topic

Just as you have done for paragraphs, you often need to narrow a general essay topic to a smaller one.

Because essays are longer than paragraphs, essay topics can be a little more general than paragraph topics, but not a lot more. The topic still needs to be narrow enough that you can make your main point about it in a manageable number of paragraphs. Use prewriting (see Chapter 2) to narrow and explore your topic as necessary.

The following examples show how the topic for an essay is a little broader than one for a paragraph.

ASSIGNED GENERAL TOPIC		NARROWED FOR AN ESSAY		NARROWED FOR A PARAGRAPH
Student stress	→	Managing work and college	→	Studying for a test
Television programs	→	Reality TV	→	*American Idol*
Gender differences	→	Male/female speech patterns	→	Male/female responses to a James Bond movie

PRACTICE 1

Narrow the following five general topics to good essay topics. Think about whether you could make a point about the topic and support that point in three paragraphs.

1. Professional sports

2. Vacation

3. Personal goals

4. Helping others

5. Things that annoy you

As you narrow your topic, you usually get some ideas about why that topic is important to you (or what is interesting about it) and what you want to say about it. Make a note of those ideas so that you can use them to write a thesis statement.

Write a Thesis Statement

The **thesis statement** of an essay is similar to the topic sentence of a paragraph. It usually introduces the narrowed topic that the essay will focus on, and it includes the main point of the essay in a clear and confident statement.

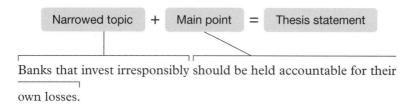

Banks that invest irresponsibly should be held accountable for their own losses.

PRACTICE 2

Write a thesis statement for each of the following essay topics. After you have written each thesis statement, circle the topic and underline the main point.

1. How drinking affects driving ability

2. Annoying things about public transportation

3. Kinds of fast-food restaurants

4. Some differences between what men like and what women like

5. Kinds of summer activities

PRACTICE 3

Write a thesis statement for each of the narrowed topics you wrote for Practice 1.

You may have to rewrite your thesis statement several times, first after you write it and again as you read and revise your essay. Because the thesis statement sets up the whole essay, it must clearly state the main point that the essay will support.

PRACTICE 4

Rewrite three of the thesis statements that you wrote for Practice 3. Think about how someone else would react to the original statement, and strongly state what you want to show, explain, or prove about your topic.

Support Your Thesis Statement and Write Topic Sentences

Each body paragraph in an essay presents a different point that supports your thesis statement. The point of each paragraph is expressed in a topic sentence. Then, the rest of the sentences in the paragraph show, explain, or prove the topic sentence.

Using a prewriting technique is an excellent way to find support. You practiced these ways to get ideas (freewriting, brainstorming, mapping or clustering, journal writing, and using the Internet) in Chapter 2. If you need to review them, go back to that chapter.

When you have completed your prewriting, read what you have written and select the ideas that will best support your thesis; you will turn these ideas into topic sentences. You also need details and examples that will show, explain, or prove the support.

. . . .

PRACTICE 5

TIP For a review of prewriting, see Chapter 2.

Use a prewriting technique to get ideas to support your thesis and explain the support. Use one of the thesis statements you wrote for Practice 4.

. . . .

PRACTICE 6

Choose three points from your prewriting that support your thesis. Turn each support point into a topic sentence, and add details that explain the topic sentences.

. . . .

Make a Plan

After you have chosen the best support for your thesis and have written topic sentences for each major support point, decide the order in which you should present the support. Three common ways to organize your ideas are time order, space order, and order of importance. For a review of these organization methods see Chapter 4. Also, you will need to think of ideas for your introduction and your conclusion.

The planning stage is a good time to think of ideas for your introduction and conclusion. The introduction includes your thesis statement and previews what you will show, explain, or prove in the rest of your essay. It should let readers know what your purpose is and make them want to read the rest of the essay. The conclusion should both remind readers of your main point and make an observation based on what you have written. For examples of an introduction and conclusion, see the essay on pages 73–74.

PRACTICE 7

Using your work from Practices 4 and 6, fill in the blanks that follow. For each topic sentence, write sentences for the supporting details. At the top, indicate what order of organization you are using and why.

Order of organization: _____

Reason for using this order: _____

Thesis statement: _____

    Other ideas for introductory paragraph: _____

_____

Topic sentence 1: _____

    Supporting details (1 sentence for each detail): _____

_____

Topic sentence 2: _____

    Supporting details (1 sentence for each detail): _____

_____

Topic sentence 3: _____

    Supporting details (1 sentence for each detail): _____

_____

Conclusion reminding readers of main point and making an

observation: _____

Write, Revise, and Edit

The next step is to write your essay, using the outline you created and referring to the following basics of a good draft. Make sure to indent each paragraph. (If you are using a computer, you can do this with the tab key.)

Four Basics of a Good Draft

1 It has an introduction that gets readers interested and includes a thesis statement.

2 It has a topic sentence for each paragraph supporting the thesis.

3 It has examples and details to support each topic sentence.

4 It has a conclusion that reminds readers of the main point and makes an observation.

PRACTICE 8

Using your outline from Practice 7, write a draft essay.

Get feedback on your draft by asking another student to answer the Questions for a Peer Reviewer checklist on page 32. After taking a break, reread your draft essay, thinking about the feedback you received.

PRACTICE 9

Revise your draft, using the following checklist as a guide.

CHECKLIST

Evaluating your essay

- ☐ My essay fulfills the assignment and includes all of the Four Basics of a Good Draft (p. 79).

- ☐ My writing style is appropriate for the audience and purpose. (Most college assignments should be written in formal English.)

- ☐ In the introduction, my thesis statement expresses my main point with confidence.

- ☐ The body paragraphs have good topic sentences that support the thesis statement.

- ☐ Detailed examples show, explain, or prove the points made in the topic sentences.

- ☐ The paragraphs are organized logically, and I have included transitions to move readers smoothly from one idea to the next.

- ☐ My concluding paragraph reminds readers of my main point and ends on a strong note.

- ☐ I have reread the essay, making improvements and checking for grammar and spelling errors.

7

The Parts of Speech

A Brief Review

Nouns

A **noun** is a word that names a general or specific person, place, thing, or idea. Nouns that name a specific person, place, thing, or idea need to begin with capital letters.

	GENERAL (COMMON NOUNS)	SPECIFIC (PROPER NOUNS)
Person	politician	Barack H. Obama
Place	city	Chicago
Thing	shoe	Nike
Idea	peace	Nobel Peace Prize

Most nouns can be **singular**, meaning *one*, or **plural**, meaning *more than one*.

SINGULAR	PLURAL	SINGULAR	PLURAL	
politician	politicians	dish	dishes	**TIP** For rules and instructions on how to form plural nouns, see Chapter 14.
window	windows	tax	taxes	
apple	apples	city	cities	
shoe	shoes	key	keys	
bus	buses	wife	wives	
man	men	tooth	teeth	

✓ **LearningCurve** For extra practice in the skills covered in this chapter, visit **bedfordstmartins.com/rsinteractive**.

Pronouns

Pronouns replace nouns or other pronouns in a sentence so that you do not have to repeat them.

Earl loaned me ~~Earl's~~ *his* lawn mower.

[The pronoun *his* replaces *Earl's*.]

You know Tina. ~~Tina~~ *She* is my best friend.

[The pronoun *she* replaces *Tina*.]

After ~~the singers'~~ *their* final performance, the singers celebrated.

[The pronoun *their* replaces *the singers'*.]

The noun or pronoun that a pronoun replaces is called the **antecedent**. In many cases, a pronoun refers to a specific antecedent nearby.

Antecedent

I removed my photo albums and papers from the basement. It flooded just an hour later.

Pronoun replacing antecedent

Personal Pronouns

Personal pronouns take the place of specific persons or things.

Singer Amy Winehouse died young. She was only twenty-seven years old.

The Boston Bruins won the Stanley Cup in 2011. They had not won it since 1972.

When rescuers found the young boy, his pulse was weak.

Personal pronouns may not have an antecedent if the meaning is clear.

I remember seeing that movie last summer.

It was very thoughtful of the class to send you flowers.

That laptop is mine.

Our project took three weeks to finish.

Personal pronouns can act like nouns, serving as the subjects or objects in a sentence, or they can be possessives, describing the ownership of a noun.

Personal Pronouns

	SUBJECT		OBJECT		POSSESSIVE	
	Singular	Plural	Singular	Plural	Singular	Plural
First Person	I	we	me	us	my/mine	our/ours
Second Person	you	you	you	you	your/yours	your/yours
Third Person	he she it	they	him her it	them	his her/hers its	their/theirs

SUBJECT PRONOUNS

A **subject pronoun** serves as the subject, or the main noun, that does the action of a verb.

She plays on the softball team.

I changed the oil.

We ate the cake.

OBJECT PRONOUNS

An **object pronoun** either receives the action of the verb (it is the object of the verb) or is part of a prepositional phrase (it is the object of the preposition).

OBJECT OF THE VERB	Roberto asked me to copy the report.
	[*Me* receives the action of the verb *asked*.]
	Roberto gave me the report.
	[*Me* receives the action of the verb *gave*.]
OBJECT OF THE PREPOSITION	Roberto gave the report to me.
	[*Me* is part of the prepositional phrase *to me*.]

POSSESSIVE PRONOUNS

Possessive pronouns refer to an antecedent and show that antecedent's ownership of something.

The students will choose their class president on Tuesday.

[The antecedent of the pronoun *their* is *students;* the president belongs to the students.]

Denise left her watch at the hotel.

[The antecedent of the pronoun *her* is *Denise;* the watch belongs to Denise.]

As with all personal pronouns, possessives may not have an antecedent if the meaning is clear.

My handwriting is hard to read.

[The handwriting belongs to me; no antecedent is needed.]

The winning project was ours.

[The project belongs to us; no antecedent is needed.]

Because possessive pronouns already show ownership, you never need to put an apostrophe in them.

INCORRECT	That job is *your's.*
CORRECT	That job is *yours.*

Indefinite Pronouns

An **indefinite pronoun** does not refer to a specific person, place, thing, or idea, so it does not have an antecedent. Most indefinite pronouns function only as nouns (subjects or objects).

Someone in the audience was smoking.

Everyone clapped when the bride and groom were announced.

The volunteers are not allowed to accept anything for their work.

Some indefinite pronouns can function either as nouns or as adjectives describing a noun.

All are welcome to join the club.

All classes were canceled because of the fire.

Few could argue with the judge's decision.

The mechanic had seen few cars as run-down as mine.

Indefinite Pronouns

all	everybody	nobody
another	everyone	none
any	everything	nothing
anybody	few	one
anyone	many	several
anything	most	some
both	much	somebody
each	neither	someone
either	no one	something

Other Types of Pronouns

REFLEXIVE AND INTENSIVE PRONOUNS

Reflexive pronouns are used when the person receiving the action is the same as the actor in the sentence. They end with the suffix -*self* or -*selves*.

Louis taught himself how to speak Italian.

We forced ourselves to study on weekends.

Intensive pronouns also end with -*self* or -*selves*, but they are used to emphasize the noun or pronoun being referenced.

The queen herself would envy my grandmother's herb garden.

The billionaires themselves have offered to pay higher taxes.

Intensive/Reflexive Pronouns

	SINGULAR	PLURAL
First Person	myself	ourselves
Second Person	yourself	yourselves
Third Person	herself himself itself	themselves

RELATIVE PRONOUNS

Relative pronouns refer to a noun already mentioned in a sentence, and they introduce a group of words that describe that noun.

The chef who wins the competition will receive $10,000.
[Which chef? The one who wins the competition.]

Basketball, which was invented in 1891, is my favorite sport.
[How is basketball being described? As a sport invented in 1891.]

The house that was almost torn down is now a historic landmark.
[Which house? The one that was almost torn down.]

Relative Pronouns	
who	which
whom	that
whose	

INTERROGATIVE PRONOUNS

Interrogative pronouns are used to begin questions.

Which sport was invented in 1891?

What was the jury's verdict?

Whom were you speaking to?

Interrogative Pronouns	
who	which
whom	what
whose	

DEMONSTRATIVE PRONOUNS

Demonstrative pronouns specify which noun is being referred to.

This restaurant looks better than that one across the street.

Use these new dishes, not those old ones.

Verbs

All sentences have at least one **verb** that explains the action or state of being of a noun.

I drive to school.

The car is black.

Verbs can change form depending on the subject (see Chapter 11, Subject-Verb Agreement Problems).

I drive to school every day, but Shane drives only one day a week.

Verbs also change tense depending on when the action took place (see Chapter 12, Verb-Tense Problems).

I walk to school every day this year, but last year I walked only once.

Action Verbs

Action verbs show the subject *doing* something.

My mother calls me at least three times per week.

On Saturdays, Maya feeds the ducks by the river.

Last year, we hiked Mount Washington.

Linking Verbs

Linking verbs connect the subject of the sentence to a word or words that describe it.

Even fake fur coats feel soft.

Jose looked older with a beard.

The children are quiet this morning.

Some words can be either action verbs or linking verbs, depending on how they are used.

ACTION VERB   Mario tasted the lasagna.

[Mario *does* something: he *tasted* the lasagna.]

LINKING VERB   The lasagna tasted delicious.

[The lasagna doesn't *do* anything. *Tasted* links lasagna to a word that describes it: *delicious.*]

Common Linking Verbs

FORMS OF *BE*	FORMS OF *BECOME* AND *SEEM*	FORMS OF SENSE VERBS
am are is was were	become/becomes/became seem/seems/seemed	appear/appears/appeared feel/feels/felt look/looks/looked smell/smells/smelled taste/tastes/tasted

---

Main Verbs and Helping Verbs

A complete verb may consist of more than one part: a **main verb** and a **helping verb**. In the sentences below, the complete verbs are double-underlined, and the helping verbs are circled.

I am driving to school right now.

Mauricio might call this evening.

They will be eating lunch at 12:00.

In questions or negative sentences, some words may interrupt the helping verb and the main verb.

Did you wait for the bell to ring?

Chloe has not studied for two days.

Common Helping Verbs

FORMS OF *BE*	FORMS OF *HAVE*	FORMS OF *DO*	OTHER
be am are been being is was were	have has had	do does did	can could may might must shall should will would

Adjectives

Adjectives describe nouns and pronouns. They add information about what kind, which one, or how many.

The five new students shared a two-floor house.

The funny movie made the sad little girls laugh.

Two large gray birds stood in the water.

Adjectives can come either before or after the nouns that they describe.

Many inexpensive homes are for sale in that area.

The homes for sale in that area are inexpensive.

Sometimes words that look like nouns act like adjectives.

The computer technician repaired Shania's laptop.

Adverbs

Adverbs describe verbs, adjectives, or other adverbs. They add information about how, how much, when, where, or why. Adverbs often end with -*ly*.

DESCRIBING A VERB	Mira sings beautifully. [*Beautifully* describes the verb *sings*.]
DESCRIBING AN ADJECTIVE	The extremely talented singer entertained the crowd. [*Extremely* describes the adjective *talented*.]
DESCRIBING ANOTHER ADVERB	Mira sings very beautifully. [*Very* describes the adverb *beautifully*.]

Like adjectives, adverbs can come either before or after the words they modify, and more than one adverb can be used to modify a word.

Prepositions

A **preposition** is a word (such as *of, above, between, about*) that comes before a noun or pronoun and helps show how that noun or pronoun relates to another part of a sentence. The group of words in combination with the preposition is called a **prepositional phrase**.

> The cow jumped (over) the moon.
>
> [*Over* is the preposition; *over the moon* is the prepositional phrase describing where the cow jumped.]
>
> When you observe an unusual event, you should write (about) it.
>
> [*About* is the preposition; *about it* is the prepositional phrase describing what you should write. (The pronoun *it* refers to *event*.)]

The prepositional phrase may contain more than one noun or pronoun, and it contains all the adjectives related to those nouns or pronouns.

> I quit school and joined a rock band (against) my parents' will.
>
> After a year (of) all work and no play, I finally got my diploma.

Sentences may contain several prepositional phrases, sometimes in a row.

> The pendant dangled (from) a shiny gold chain (with) a small diamond (in) each link.

Common Prepositions

about	before	except	of	to
above	behind	for	off	toward
across	below	from	on	under
after	beneath	in	out	until
against	beside	inside	outside	up
along	between	into	over	upon
among	by	like	past	with
around	down	near	since	within
at	during	next to	through	without

Note that even though the word *to* can be a preposition, it is often used as part of a verb's infinitive: *to walk, to run, to drive*. These are not prepositional phrases, and the word *to* is not a preposition when it is used in an infinitive.

Conjunctions

Conjunctions are used to connect words and word groups. There are two main types of conjunctions: coordinating and subordinating.

Coordinating Conjunctions

Coordinating conjunctions join two or more words or word groups that have the same function in a sentence.

Dogs (and) cats are common household pets.

[The conjunction *and* joins the two nouns *dogs* and *cats*.]

I knew I would have to drop a class, quit the swim team, (or) cut back on work.

[The conjunction *or* joins the three phrases *drop a class*, *quit the swim team*, and *cut back on work*.]

The semester begins tomorrow, (but) the school is still under construction.

[The conjunction *but* joins two complete thoughts: *The semester begins tomorrow* and *the school is still under construction*.]

Remember the seven coordinating conjunctions by using the acronym *fan-boys:* (**f**or, **a**nd, **n**or, **b**ut, **o**r, **y**et, **s**o).

Coordinating Conjunctions						
for	and	nor	but	or	yet	so

Subordinating Conjunctions (Dependent Words)

Subordinating conjunctions are words that help explain when or under what circumstances an event occurred.

(When) Sam opened the refrigerator, he smelled the moldy cheese.

The smell was overwhelming (when) Sam opened the refrigerator.

In this book, subordinating conjunctions are also called **dependent words** because they can turn a complete thought (or an independent clause) into an incomplete thought (or a dependent clause).

Sam opened the refrigerator.

[The words above form a complete thought.]

(When) Sam opened the refrigerator

[The addition of the dependent word *when* makes the thought incomplete. (What happened when Sam opened the refrigerator?)]

Common Subordinating Conjunctions (Dependent Words)

after	if	what(ever)
although	since	when(ever)
as	so that	where(ver)
because	that	whether
before	though	which
even though	unless	while
how	until	who/whose

Interjections

Interjections are words that show excitement or emotion. They are not typically used in formal English.

(Oh,) did you need that report today?

(Wow!) This is the best cupcake I ever tasted!

8

Complete Sentences

Key Parts to Know

Understand What a Sentence Is

A **sentence** is the basic unit of written communication. A complete sentence in formal English has a **subject** and a **verb** and expresses a **complete thought**. Sentences are also called **independent clauses** because they make sense by themselves, without other information.

None of the following examples is a sentence:

Invented the telephone in 1876.

The Great Wall of China the largest man-made structure in the world.

The movie *Slumdog Millionaire*, which won several Oscars.[1]

The first example is missing a subject, the second is missing a verb, and none express a complete thought. Here they are rewritten as complete sentences:

Alexander Graham Bell **invented** the telephone in 1876.

The Great Wall of China *is* the largest man-made structure in the world.

The movie *Slumdog Millionaire*, which won several Oscars, *is about a young Indian boy.*

[1] **Oscars:** Film-industry awards given every year in the categories of best movie, best actor, best screenwriter, and others.

Subjects

A **subject** is the word or words that a sentence is about. Subjects can be **nouns** (people—Alexander Graham Bell; places—the Great Wall of China; things—the movie *Slumdog Millionaire*). They can also be **pronouns** (like *I, you, he/she, it, we, they*).

✓ **LearningCurve** For extra practice in the skills covered in this chapter, visit bedfordstmartins.com/rsinteractive.

TIP For more on nouns, see Chapter 7.

Subject Nouns

The **noun as subject** is the person, place, thing, or idea that either performs the action or is the main focus of the sentence. In the examples in this chapter, subjects appear in bold light green.

> Janine **tripped** on the sidewalk.
>
> [Janine performs the action, *tripped*.]

> Carlo **looked** great in his new glasses.
>
> [Carlo is the focus of the sentence.]

Subject Pronouns

TIP For more on pronouns, see Chapter 7.

Like a noun subject, the **subject pronoun** is the person, place, thing, or idea that performs the action or is the main focus of the sentence. The subject pronouns are *I, you* (singular), *he, she, it, we, you* (plural), and *they.*

Simple and Complete Subjects

A **simple subject** is just the one noun or pronoun that the sentence is about.

> The summer-school **students were taking** final exams.

A **complete subject** includes all the words that describe the simple subject.

> The summer-school **students were taking** final exams.

Singular and Plural Subjects

Singular means one, and *plural* means more than one. Sentences can have singular or plural subjects.

> **SINGULAR**   Elizabeth Blackwell **was** the first woman doctor in the United States.
>
> [There is one noun: *Elizabeth Blackwell*.]

> **PLURAL**   Elizabeth Blackwell and her sister Emily **were** both doctors.
>
> [There are two separate nouns: *Elizabeth Blackwell* and *her sister Emily*.]

> The Blackwell sisters **started** a women's medical college in the late 1800s.
>
> [There is one plural noun: *The Blackwell sisters*.]

Prepositional Phrases

A common mistake is to think that the subject of the sentence is in a **prepositional phrase**, which starts with a **preposition** and ends with a noun (the object of the preposition).

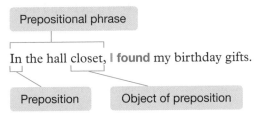

Prepositional phrase

In the hall closet, I **found** my birthday gifts.

Preposition   Object of preposition

You might think that the words *hall closet* are the subject of the sentence, but—*and this is very important*—**the subject of a sentence is never in a prepositional phrase**.

TIP For a list of common prepositions, see p. 90.

To find prepositional phrases, look for prepositions. To make sure that you do not confuse the noun in the prepositional phrase (the object of the preposition) with the subject of the sentence, try crossing out the prepositional phrase.

~~In the hall closet,~~ I **found** my birthday gifts.

Many sentences have more than one prepositional phrase. To find the subject, cross out all the prepositional phrases.

~~At the Apollo Theater~~ ~~in New York City,~~ many famous African American musicians **got** their start.

Some ~~of the big future stars~~ **were** Count Basie, Billie Holiday, Ella Fitzgerald, and Aretha Franklin.

~~In the 1970s,~~ ~~after some years~~ ~~of slow business,~~ the theater **closed**.

~~After major remodeling,~~ the theater **reopened** ~~in 1985~~.

Verbs

Every sentence has a **verb** that either tells what the subject does or connects the subject to another word that describes it. In the examples in this chapter, the subject's verb is shown in bold dark green.

For a review of what a verb is, see Chapter 7.

Clarence Birdseye **invented** frozen foods in 1923.

[The verb *invented* tells what Birdseye, the subject, did.]

By 1930, he **was** ready to sell his product.

[The verb *was* connects the subject to a word that describes him: *ready*.]

Action verbs show the subject *doing* something.

The **players** **dumped** the cooler of ice water on their coach's head.

Linking verbs connect the subject of the sentence to a word or words that describe it. In the following sentence, the linking verb is bold and the words describing the subject are in italics.

Joseph McCarthy **was** *a powerful senator from Wisconsin.*

Helping verbs are joined with main verbs to make a complete verb.

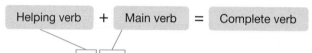

Thumbelina **can hold** her breath for one hundred seconds.
[*Can* is the helping verb, and *hold* is the main verb.]

Complete Thoughts

Even when a group of words has a subject and a verb, it may not express a complete thought.

Because their **team** **won** the championship.
[There is a subject (*team*) and a verb (*won*), but you cannot tell what is going on without more information.]

In the following examples, the added words (in italics) create a complete thought.

The **students** **went** *wild* because their team won the championship.

Because their team won the championship, *the* **students** **went** *wild.*

Read the following sentences and ask if there is a complete thought.

Who **sat** next to me in class.

Damon **saved** the game.

TIP For more on dependent clauses, see Chapter 14. A word group that has a subject and a verb but that is not a complete thought is called a **dependent clause**. It is not a sentence because it is *dependent* on another set of words for meaning.

Six Basic English Sentence Patterns

In English, there are six basic sentence patterns, some of which you have already studied in this chapter. Although there are other patterns, they build on these six.

1. Subject-Verb (S-V)

Dogs **bark**.

2. Subject-Linking Verb-Noun (S-LV-N)

They **are** animals.

3. Subject-Linking Verb-Adjective (S-LV-ADJ)

Cats **seem** quiet.

4. Subject-Verb-Adverb (S-V-ADV)

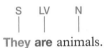

They **meow** softly.

5. Subject-Verb-Direct Object (S-V-DO)

A *direct object* directly receives the action of the verb.

Dogs **fetch** sticks.

6. Subject-Verb-Indirect Object-Direct Object (S-V-IO-DO)

An *indirect object* does not directly receive the action of the verb.

My **dog brings** me sticks.

Longer Sentences

Compound Sentences

A **compound sentence** contains two complete thoughts (**independent clauses**), usually joined by a comma and a coordinating conjunction (*and, but, for, nor, or, so, yet*).

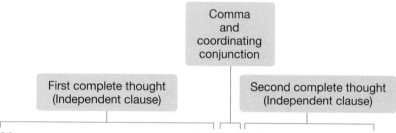

My son got a new computer yesterday, and he is using it right now.

You can remember the coordinating conjunctions by thinking of *fanboys:* **f**or, **a**nd, **n**or, **b**ut, **o**r, **y**et, **s**o.

In a compound sentence, the complete thoughts being joined are related, and they are equal in importance.

Texting is a great way to stay in touch with friends, and it is fun.

I wanted to go swimming after work, but the pool was closed.

You can drive to work with me, or you can wait for the bus.

Complex Sentences

TIP For a list of common dependent words, see page 92.

A **complex sentence** contains two ideas, but one of those ideas is dependent on (or subordinate to) the other. The complete thought (also called the **independent clause**) can stand on its own as a sentence, but the dependent idea (also called a **dependent clause** or a **subordinate clause**) cannot. The dependent clause begins with a dependent word (also called a **subordinating conjunction**) such as *after, although, because,* or *when.*

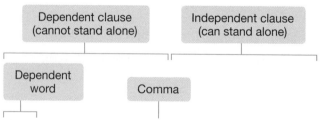

When I had food poisoning, my friends were supportive.

The dependent clause can come before or after the independent clause. Note that when the independent clause comes before the dependent clause, no comma is used to join the two sentences.

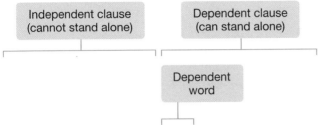

My friends were supportive **when** I had food poisoning.

After I raked the entire yard, I was tired.

You must drive with an adult **even though** you have your driver's license.

If Patti works overtime, she will make an extra $200 this week.

Compound-Complex Sentences

A **compound-complex sentence** is a compound sentence (two or more independent clauses) that also has one or more dependent clauses.

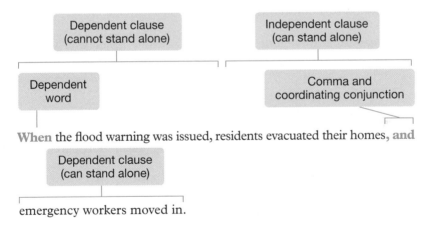

When the flood warning was issued, residents evacuated their homes, **and**

emergency workers moved in.

The dependent clause(s) can come before or after the independent clauses.

Residents evacuated their homes, **and** emergency workers moved in **when** the flood warning was issued.

9

Fragments

Sentences That Are Missing a Key Part

Chapters 9 through 12 focus on four major grammar errors that people most often notice in writing.

THE FOUR MOST SERIOUS ERRORS

1. Fragments (Chapter 9)
2. Run-ons and comma splices (Chapter 10)
3. Subject-verb agreement problems (Chapter 11)
4. Verb-tense problems (Chapter 12)

TIP For a review of the parts of speech and basic sentence structure, see Chapters 7 and 8.

If you can avoid these four—just four—kinds of errors, your writing will improve.

Understand What Fragments Are

A **fragment** is a group of words that is missing one or more parts of a complete sentence.

FRAGMENT	To the store.
	[*Who* is doing *what?* You cannot tell without more information.]
SENTENCE	Dara <u>drove</u> to the store.
	[A subject, *Dara*, and an action verb, *drove*, make the fragment a complete sentence. Now you know *who did what*.]

Read the following word groups, pausing at the periods. Is there a difference in the way you read the fragment (in italics) and the sentence? If you read only the words in italics, would they be a complete thought?

| FRAGMENT | I am going to a concert on Friday. *At Memorial Arena.* |
| SENTENCE | I am going to a concert on Friday at Memorial Arena. |

| FRAGMENT | Jack loves Florida. *Because it is warm.* |
| SENTENCE | Jack loves Florida because it is warm. |

| FRAGMENT | Penny broke her leg. *Snowboarding last week.* |
| SENTENCE | Penny broke her leg snowboarding last week. |

TIP In the sentence examples in this chapter, subjects are underlined and verbs are double-underlined.

The following section explains how to find and fix five common types of fragments.

Find and Correct Fragments

Trouble Spot 1: Fragments That Start with a Prepositional Phrase

Check your writing for sentences that start with prepositions. You may find a fragment.

| FRAGMENT | The groom sneezed ten times. (During) the wedding. |

If a subject or verb is missing or if there is not a complete thought, that is a fragment. [The word group in this example is a fragment: It does not have a subject, a verb, or a complete thought.]

Correct the fragment by connecting it to the sentence either before or after it. Or, make the fragment into its own sentence.

CORRECTED	The groom sneezed ten times/ During the wedding.
	He sneezed during the wedding.
CORRECTED	The groom sneezed ten times. ~~During the wedding.~~

TIP For a list of common prepositions, see page 90.

If the prepositional phrase comes first, a comma must follow it.

During the wedding, the groom sneezed ten times.

PREPOSITIONAL-PHRASE FRAGMENTS

Last week, I found a starfish. *At the beach.*

Free parking is available. *Behind the mall.*

FRAGMENT JOINED TO SENTENCES

Last week, I found a starfish at the beach.

Free parking is available behind the mall.

PREPOSITIONAL-PHRASE FRAGMENTS

I visited the Super Duper Dollar Store. *In the Emerald Square Mall.*

I am taking a three-week luxury cruise with Carnival Cruise Lines. *With my mother.*

FRAGMENTS MADE INTO THEIR OWN SENTENCES

I visited the Super Duper Dollar Store. It is in the Emerald Square Mall.

I am taking a three-week luxury cruise with Carnival Cruise Lines. My mother is coming along.

The word groups in italics have no subject (remember that the subject is *never* in the prepositional phrase). Also, they have no verb and no complete thought.

- -

PRACTICE 1

In the following paragraph, eight of the ten items include a fragment that starts with a prepositional phrase. Underline each fragment, and then correct it either by adding the missing sentence elements or by connecting it to the previous or the next sentence. Two items are correct; write **C** next to them.

1 You should wait for a while before going swimming. After a meal.
2 Most of us have heard this warning since we were young. We might

even repeat it to our own children. **3** At the pool. Children wait impatiently for their food to digest. **4** They take the warning seriously, believing that muscle cramps caused by food might lead to drowning. **5** From a review of the available statistics. It now appears that this warning is a myth. **6** Of drownings in the United States. Less than 1 percent occurred right after the victim ate a meal, according to one study. **7** With alcohol use involved. The story is different. **8** Among one hundred drowning deaths in the state of Washington one year. Twenty-five percent had been drinking heavily. **9** In California. Forty-one percent of drowning deaths one year were alcohol-related. **10** So you should no longer be afraid of swimming after eating, unless you had some alcohol. With your meal.

Trouble Spot 2: Fragments That Start with a Dependent Word

Watch for word groups that begin with a dependent word such as *although, because,* or *unless.* You might find a fragment.

TIP For a list of common dependent words (subordinating conjunctions), see page 92.

FRAGMENT   Do not get me anything from the bakery. (Unless) you

see something with a lot of chocolate.

If a subject or verb is missing or if there is not a complete thought, it is a fragment. [The word group in this example is a fragment: It has a subject and a verb, but it is not a complete thought.]

Correct the fragment by connecting it to the sentence either before or after it. Or, make the fragment into its own sentence.

CORRECTED   Do not get me anything from the bakery. *u*Unless you

see something with a lot of chocolate.

CORRECTED   Do not get me anything from the bakery. ~~Unless~~ *However,*

if you see something with a lot of chocolate,
~~you see something with a lot of chocolate.~~
ignore these instructions.

If the dependent word group comes first, a comma must follow it.

Unless you see something with a lot of chocolate, do not get me anything from the bakery.

DEPENDENT-WORD FRAGMENTS

Amy got to the club. *After I went home.*

She went home to change. *Because she was uncomfortable.*

FRAGMENTS JOINED TO A SENTENCE

Amy got to the club after I went home.

She went home to change because she was uncomfortable.

DEPENDENT-WORD FRAGMENTS

I went to the Web site of IBM. *Since that is the company I want to work for.*

Rob is known for having tantrums at airports. *Whenever his flight is delayed.*

FRAGMENTS MADE INTO THEIR OWN SENTENCES

I went to the Web site of IBM. Since that is the company I want to work for, I want to gather as much information about it as possible.

Rob is known for having tantrums at airports. He gets upset whenever his flight is delayed.

The word groups in italics have a subject and a verb, but they do not make sense alone; they are **dependent**, meaning that they depend on other words for their meaning. They are called *dependent clauses.*

· ·

PRACTICE 2

All but one of the numbered items in the following paragraph include a fragment that begins with a dependent word. Underline the fragments, and then correct them either by adding the missing sentence elements or by connecting them to the previous or the next sentence. Write **C** next to the one correct item.

1 Because my cousin majored in zoology. He knows a lot about animals. **2** He was also an Eagle Scout. Which means he is familiar with many outdoor survival techniques. **3** He says that many people have an irrational fear of snakes. Even though most snakes are quite harmless.

4 Usually a snake will avoid contact. If it hears someone approaching.
5 Whenever most people see a snake. They freeze. **6** If a person does get bitten by a snake. It probably is not a deadly bite. **7** Although a shot of antivenom is probably not needed. It is a good idea to call 911 and get to the nearest hospital just in case. **8** It is also a good idea to remember what the snake looked like. Since the doctors and animal-control workers will want a description of it. **9** A snake bite can certainly be scary. However, remember that only six people die from snake bites in the United States each year.

Trouble Spot 3: Fragments That Start with an *-ing* Verb

Check your writing for sentences that begin with a verb ending in *-ing*. You might find a fragment.

FRAGMENT   Charlie stood on his toes in the crowd. (Trying) to see the passing parade.

If a subject or verb is missing or if there is not a complete thought, it is a fragment. [The word group in this example is a fragment: It does not have a subject, and it is not a complete thought.]
    Correct the fragment by making it into its own sentence. Or, connect the fragment to the sentence either before or after it.

                                           He was trying
CORRECTED   Charlie stood on his toes in the crowd. ~~Trying~~ to see
                                           ^
the passing parade.

Usually, you will need to put a comma before or after the fragment to join it to the complete sentence.

              Trying to see the passing parade,
CORRECTED   Charlie stood on his toes in the crowd. ~~Trying to see~~
              ^
~~the passing parade.~~

-ING VERB FRAGMENTS

I will be up late tonight. *Studying for finals.*

I get plenty of daily exercise. *Walking to the bus stop.*

FRAGMENTS JOINED TO SENTENCES

I will be up late tonight studying for finals.

I get plenty of daily exercise walking to the bus stop.

-*ING* VERB FRAGMENTS

Gerard swims for three hours each day. *Training for the regionals.*

Maya took a plane instead of the bus. *Wanting to get home as fast as possible.*

FRAGMENTS MADE INTO THEIR OWN SENTENCES

Gerard swims for three hours each day. He is training for the regionals.

Maya took a plane instead of the bus. She wanted to get home as fast as possible.

. . . .

PRACTICE 3

In the following paragraph, eight items include a fragment that begins with an *-ing* verb form. Underline any fragment, and then correct it either by adding the missing sentence elements or by connecting it to the previous or the next sentence. Write **C** next to the two correct items.

1 Tens of millions of Americans try online dating every year. Making it one of the most popular paid services on the Internet. **2** Three economists recently researched an online dating service. Revealing some interesting facts. **3** Filling out a personal profile is one of the first steps in online dating. The information that people provide is often hard to believe. **4** Describing their appearance. Only 1 percent of those studied said their looks were less than average. **5** Looks were the most important personal feature. Ranking first for both women and men. **6** Hearing this fact. Most people are not surprised. **7** Women who posted photos got higher interest. Receiving twice as many e-mail responses as those who did not post photos. **8** Having plenty of money seems to increase men's chances of finding a date. Men who reported high incomes received nearly twice the e-mail responses as men with low incomes. **9** Going beyond looks

and income. Most relationships last because of the personalities involved.
10 Accepting online dating despite some participants' focus on looks
and money. Many single people say that it is no worse than other ways of
meeting people.

Trouble Spot 4: Fragments That Start with *to* and a Verb

Check your writing for sentences that begin with *to* and a verb. You may
find a fragment.

FRAGMENT   We went to at least five music stores. To find the guitar

that Colin wanted.

If a subject or verb is missing or if there is not a complete thought,
there is a fragment. [The word group in this example is a fragment: It does
not have a subject, and it is not a complete thought.]

Correct the fragment by connecting it to the sentence either before or
after it. Or, make the fragment into its own sentence.

CORRECTED   We went to at least five music stores, to find the guitar

that Colin wanted.

CORRECTED   We went to at least five music stores. It took us a long time to find the guitar

that Colin wanted.

Word groups consisting only of *to* and a verb are also called **infinitives**.
They do not function as verbs.

TO + VERB FRAGMENTS

Christiane went home last week. *To help her mother move.*

Hundreds of people were waiting in line. *To get tickets.*

FRAGMENTS JOINED TO SENTENCES

Christiane went home last week to help her mother move.

Hundreds of people were waiting in line to get tickets.

TO + VERB FRAGMENTS

<u>Barry</u> <u>spent</u> an hour on the phone waiting. *To talk to a customer-service representative.*

<u>Leah</u> <u>wrote</u> several letters to politicians. *To build support for the pedestrian-rights bill.*

FRAGMENTS MADE INTO THEIR OWN SENTENCES

<u>Barry</u> <u>spent</u> an hour on the phone waiting. <u>He</u> <u>wanted</u> to talk to a customer-service representative.

<u>Leah</u> <u>wrote</u> several letters to politicians. <u>She</u> <u>hoped</u> to build support for the pedestrian-rights bill.

- -

PRACTICE 4

In the following paragraph, most items include a fragment that begins with an infinitive (*to* + a verb). Underline any fragment and then correct it either by adding the missing sentence elements or by connecting it to the previous or next sentence. Two items are correct; write **C** next to them.

1 To make cars more comfortable and convenient to drive. Engineers have designed many high-tech features. **2** Seat heaters were invented. To keep people warm while driving in cold weather. **3** However, some seat heaters are programmed. To switch off after fifteen minutes without warning the driver. **4** To stay warm on a long trip. The driver must remember to keep turning the seat heater back on. **5** To some people, these cars may be too convenient. One car's computer has seven hundred possible commands. **6** To avoid bothering their neighbors at night. Some people want to stop their cars from honking when they lock the doors. **7** Many people do not know that it is fairly easy. To turn off some of a car's features. **8** Some people carefully study their cars' systems. To change the programming. **9** To make programming changes on one's own car is risky. It may cause the car's warranty to be lost. **10** It is probably easiest for people who own these complicated cars. To simply enjoy their high-tech conveniences.

- -

Trouble Spot 5: Fragments That Start with an Example or Explanation

Check your writing for sentences that begin with an example or explanation. Look for words like *especially, for example, for instance, like,* and *such as.* You may find a fragment.

FRAGMENT I can tell you about a lot of bad dates I had. Like the one when I was taken to a funeral.

If a subject or verb is missing or if there is not a complete thought, it is a fragment. [The word group in this example is a fragment: It has a subject and a verb, but it is not a complete thought.]

Correct the fragment by connecting it to the sentence either before or after it. Or, make the fragment into its own sentence.

CORRECTED I can tell you about a lot of bad dates I had, Like the one when I was taken to a funeral.

CORRECTED I can tell you about a lot of bad dates I had. ~~Like~~ *The* ~~the~~ one when I was taken to a funeral, *was especially memorable.*

When you add a fragment to a complete sentence, you may need to add a comma, as in the first corrected example.

FRAGMENTS STARTING WITH AN EXAMPLE OR EXPLANATION

I would like to get new boots. *Like the ones that Sheila wore last night.*

I get lots of offers from credit card companies. *Such as Visa and MasterCard.*

FRAGMENTS JOINED TO SENTENCES

I would like to get new boots like the ones that Sheila wore last night.

I get lots of offers from credit card companies such as Visa and MasterCard.

FRAGMENTS STARTING WITH AN EXAMPLE OR EXPLANATION

<u>It</u> <u>is</u> hard to stay in and study. *Especially during the summer.*

Some <u>people</u> <u>cook</u> entirely from scratch, even if it takes all day. *For example, Bill.*

FRAGMENTS MADE INTO THEIR OWN SENTENCES

<u>It</u> <u>is</u> hard to stay in and study. <u>It</u> <u>is</u> especially hard during the summer.

Some <u>people</u> <u>cook</u> entirely from scratch, even if it takes all day. <u>Bill</u> <u>does</u> that.

PRACTICE 5

In the following paragraph, most items include a fragment that begins with an example or an explanation. Underline any fragment, and then correct it either by adding the missing sentence elements or by connecting it to the previous or the next sentence. Two items contain no fragment; write **C** next to them.

1 One major fast-food chain is making changes to its menu. Like offering fresh apple slices. **2** The company still mostly sells traditional fast food. For example, double cheeseburgers. **3** The company is trying to offer its customers healthier food. Such as fresh fruit and salads. **4** The cause of the change seems to be public opinion. Like complaints about high-calorie fast-food meals. **5** Many people are blaming fast-food companies for Americans' expanding waistlines. Especially those of children. **6** Consumers love to eat fatty foods. However, they also like to blame fast-food restaurants when they gain weight. **7** This particular restaurant is discovering that healthy food can be profitable. Such as earning about 10 percent of its income from fresh salads. **8** There are limits to how far the company will go to make its food healthier. For instance, with its apple slices. **9** Apple slices are certainly healthy. However, they are less healthy when dipped in the sugary sauce that the company packages with the slices. **10** The company followed the advice of its taste testers. For example, preferring the slices dipped in the sugary sauce.

PRACTICE 6

Read and edit the passage below, which contains many different kinds of fragments.

 1 With the increasing focus on climate change and other environmental issues. **2** Some home builders are choosing to make their homes environmentally friendly, or "green." **3** Green homes are typically planned and built very carefully. **4** With materials that are recycled, renewable, or produced in an ecologically harmless manner. **5** For example, recycled plastic decking, bamboo flooring, and chemical-free paint. **6** In addition, green homes are usually more energy efficient than traditional homes. **7** To help keep carbon emissions low. **8** Since heating and cooling a home can use up more energy than anything else in a house. **9** Green homes are usually well insulated from extreme cold or heat. **10** Their appliances also use lower-than-average amounts of water and electricity. **11** Saving both energy and money for the home owner. **12** Many green homes also have their own forms of energy production. **13** Such as solar panels or solar roof tiles that store energy for the home. **14** Some homes produce an excess of solar energy. **15** So that they can actually sell power back to the electric company. **16** Builders of green homes are doing their part to keep the planet healthy. **17** Making energy-conscious and environmentally friendly building decisions.

10

Run-Ons and Comma Splices

Two Sentences Joined Incorrectly

Understand What Run-Ons and Comma Splices Are

Sometimes, two complete **sentences** (or independent clauses) can be joined to make one sentence.

TWO COMPLETE SENTENCES JOINED CORRECTLY

Independent clause   Independent clause

TIP In the sentence examples in this chapter, subjects are underlined and verbs are double-underlined.

The bus was late, so many people went home.

Independent clause   Independent clause

Drivers were on strike, but few passengers knew it.

Complete sentences that are not joined correctly are either run-ons or comma splices. A **run-on** occurs when two complete sentences are joined without any punctuation.

Independent clause   Independent clause

RUN-ON My aunt has several dogs she has no other pets.

A **comma splice** occurs when two complete sentences are joined by only a comma instead of a comma and one of the following words: *and, but, for, nor, or, so, yet.*

Independent clause   Independent clause

COMMA SPLICE My aunt has several dogs, she has no other pets.

✓ LearningCurve For extra practice in the skills covered in this chapter, visit bedfordstmartins.com/rsinteractive.

Find and Correct Run-Ons and Comma Splices

To find run-ons and comma splices, read each sentence in your writing carefully. Underline the subjects, and double-underline the verbs.

RUN-ON   The fire spread quickly the ground was dry.

TIP Before going on in this chapter, you may want to review the following terms from Chapter 8: *sentence*, *subject*, and *verb*.

If no punctuation joins the sentences, there is a run-on. If only a comma joins the sentences, there is a comma splice.

There are three ways to fix run-ons or comma splices.

- Add a period or semicolon: *The fire spread quickly; the ground was dry.*
- Add a comma and a coordinating conjunction: *The fire spread quickly,* **for** *the ground was dry.*
- Add a subordinating conjunction (dependent word): *The fire spread quickly* **because** *the ground was dry.*

Add a Period or a Semicolon

Notice how periods and semicolons are used between complete sentences.

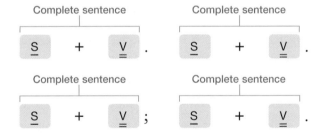

Correct a run-on or comma splice by adding a period or a semicolon.

RUN-ON   Students crowded the tiny library they were studying for final exams.

CORRECTED WITH A PERIOD   Students crowded the tiny library. They were studying for final exams.

CORRECTED WITH A SEMICOLON   Students crowded the tiny library; they were studying for final exams.

COMMA SPLICE	Children played in the park, they loved the merry-go-round.
CORRECTED WITH A PERIOD	Children played in the park. They loved the merry-go-round.
CORRECTED WITH A SEMICOLON	Children played in the park; they loved the merry-go-round.

PRACTICE 1

In the following paragraph, identify each item as a run-on (**RO**), a comma splice (**CS**), or correct (**C**) in the blank before each item. Then, correct each run-on or comma splice by adding a period or a semicolon. Capitalize letters as necessary when you make new sentences. There are four correct items.

_____ **1** People who are likable are often more successful than others. _____ **2** Being likable is an important quality no matter where you work, likable employees are often promoted over others who do their job equally well but are less pleasant to be around. _____ **3** People want to be around likable coworkers, they make everyone feel better emotionally and physically. _____ **4** According to business experts, likable employees share several characteristics. _____ **5** For example, a likable person is friendly he or she makes other people feel liked and welcome. _____ **6** One business writer suggests acting like a greeter wherever you are, you might think of yourself as a hostess welcoming guests into a party or a restaurant. _____ **7** The likable person is also sensitive to other people's wants and needs it makes people comfortable to feel understood. _____ **8** Honesty is another quality that makes a person likable. _____ **9** Most people can detect a liar, seeing through someone who is telling a lie or acting fake. _____ **10** Sincerity is important at work it is also respected in everyday dealings with others.

Add a Comma and a Coordinating Conjunction

You can add a comma and a **coordinating conjunction** between two complete sentences. Remember the seven coordinating conjunctions by using the acronym *fanboys* (**f**or, **a**nd, **n**or, **b**ut, **o**r, **y**et, **s**o).

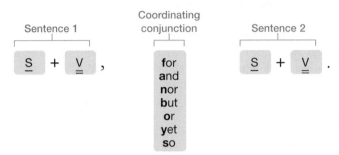

Choose the coordinating conjunction that makes sense in the sentence. (A comma splice already has a comma, so just add a coordinating conjunction.)

TIP To learn more about coordinating conjunctions, see Chapter 7.

RUN-ONS

His used <u>cars</u> <u>are</u> too expensive <u>I</u> <u>bought</u> mine from another dealer.

<u>Computers</u> <u>are</u> her first love <u>she</u> <u>spends</u> a lot of time gardening.

CORRECTED

His used <u>cars</u> <u>are</u> too expensive, *so* <u>I</u> <u>bought</u> mine from another dealer.

<u>Computers</u> <u>are</u> her first love, *yet* <u>she</u> <u>spends</u> a lot of time gardening.

COMMA SPLICES

<u>I</u> <u>would spend</u> an extra day in Chicago, <u>I</u> simply <u>do not have</u> the free time.

<u>Jane</u> <u>is</u> in charge of billing, her <u>sister</u> <u>runs</u> the lingerie department.

CORRECTED

<u>I</u> <u>would spend</u> an extra day in Chicago, *but* <u>I</u> simply <u>do not have</u> the free time.

<u>Jane</u> <u>is</u> in charge of billing, *and* her <u>sister</u> <u>runs</u> the lingerie department.

PRACTICE 2

Some items in the following paragraph are run-ons or comma splices. Correct each error by adding a comma, if necessary, and a coordinating conjunction. Two sentences are correct; write **C** next to them.

1 Bette Nesmith Graham was a secretary in the 1950s her typing skills were poor. **2** She needed more income she took a second job decorating bank windows for the holidays. **3** While painting windows, she noticed some artists painting over their mistakes. **4** She realized she could paint over her typing errors she brought a small bottle of paint to her secretarial job. **5** She soon needed more paint the other secretaries wanted to use the fluid, too. **6** She experimented with other fluids at home, she also asked her son's chemistry teacher for advice. **7** She started selling an improved fluid in 1956, she called it Mistake Out. **8** In the 1960s, she changed the name to Liquid Paper it was the same product. **9** Graham eventually sold her Liquid Paper business for $47.5 million in 1979. **10** Hardly anybody today uses a typewriter, reports show that people still use correction fluid on about 42.3 million pages a year.

Add a Subordinating Conjunction (Dependent Word)

Finally, to fix a run-on or comma splice, you can add a dependent word (also called a *subordinating conjunction*) to one of the two complete sentences to make it a dependent clause.

TIP To learn more about dependent words (subordinating conjunctions), see Chapter 7.

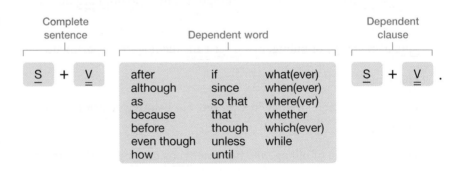

Complete sentence	Dependent word			Dependent clause
S + V	after	if	what(ever)	S + V .
	although	since	when(ever)	
	as	so that	where(ver)	
	because	that	whether	
	before	though	which(ever)	
	even though	unless	while	
	how	until		

Choose the subordinating conjunction that makes sense in the sentence.

> **RUN-ONS**
>
> Day care is free at our college I can afford to go to school.
>
> She lost her job her company outsourced her position.

> **CORRECTED**
>
> *Because* day care is free at our college, I can afford to go to school.
>
> She lost her job *after* her company outsourced her position.

> **COMMA SPLICES**
>
> He was nervous, he stayed in the delivery room.
>
> The deck will be built, they return from their vacation in June.

> **CORRECTED**
>
> *Even though* he was nervous, he stayed in the delivery room.
>
> The deck will be built *before* they return from their vacation in June.

When the dependent clause starts the sentence, add a comma after it, as in the first corrected examples in each of the previous groups. When the dependent word is in the middle of the sentence, you do not need a comma.

PRACTICE 3

In the following paragraph, correct any run-ons or comma splices by adding a subordinating conjunction. Two sentences are correct; write **C** next to them.

1 Emergency medical technicians are often the first to arrive at the scene of an emergency, they are trained to follow certain procedures. 2 The first thing they need to do is survey the scene and make sure it is safe. 3 Hazardous materials, fire, or other dangers may be present, technicians must immediately take care to protect themselves. 4 The technician carefully assesses the patient, she determines whether the patient is conscious and alert. 5 The patient shows any signs of spinal cord injuries the technician must be extra careful to prevent further damage. 6 The next

thing the technician does is look for an airway she can be sure the patient can breathe. **7** The airway is blocked, the technician must immediately find a way to unblock it. **8** The airway has been established, the technician checks to see if the patient's breathing is normal. **9** Then, the technician stops any major external bleeding and checks the patient's pulse. **10** These important initial steps have been taken, the technician can more thoroughly examine, reassure, and comfort the patient until further help can be given.

PRACTICE 4

Each of the numbered sentences below is either a run-on or a comma splice. Read and edit the passage.

    1 Xeriscaping is a form of landscaping that requires little water use, it is especially popular in dry climates. **2** Some parts of the United States often experience droughts the local governments in those areas restrict the use of sprinklers. **3** Some people in these communities are tired of seeing their lawns die each year, they have chosen to remove the lawn and install drought-resistant plants. **4** Cacti are among the most common xeriscaping plants rocks and mulch are also important elements. **5** The most popular plants in xeriscaping vary depending on the region, most drought-tolerant species are native to the location. **6** People who practice xeriscaping usually say that their yard always looks good they don't have to worry about whether or not it will rain. **7** One drawback of xeriscaping is that there is no lawn to play on it is not safe for young children to run near sharp plants or hard rocks. **8** However, many xeriscapers keep a lawn on a portion of their land the children can play there. **9** They feel that the trade-off is worth it the surrounding drought-resistant plants are strong and reliable. **10** This form of landscaping also saves home owners time and money on lawn maintenance according to most people who own them, xeriscaped lawns practically take care of themselves.

11

Subject-Verb Agreement Problems

Subjects and Verbs That Do Not Match

Understand What Subject-Verb Agreement Is

In any sentence, the **subject and the verb must match—or agree—**in number. If the subject is singular (one person, place, thing, or idea), then the verb must also be singular. If the subject is plural (more than one), the verb must also be plural.

SINGULAR	The library <u>computer</u> <u><u>crashes</u></u> often.
	[The subject, *computer,* is singular—just one computer—so the verb must take the singular form: *crashes.*]
PLURAL	The library <u>computers</u> <u><u>crash</u></u> often.
	[The subject, *computers,* is plural—more than one computer—so the verb must take the plural form: *crash.*]

TIP In the sentence examples and charts in this chapter, subjects are underlined and verbs are double-underlined.

In the present tense, verbs for third-person singular subjects (like *Bob, he, she,* or *it*) end in -*s* or -*es.*

THIRD-PERSON SINGULAR SUBJECT	PRESENT-TENSE VERB
he she it (computer)	crashes

Verbs for other subjects (*I, you, we, they*) do not add an -*s* or -*es* ending.

OTHER SUBJECTS	PRESENT-TENSE VERB
I you we they	crash

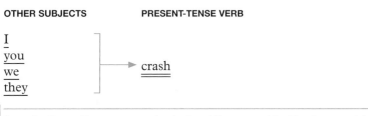

LearningCurve For extra practice in the skills covered in this chapter, visit bedfordstmartins.com/rsinteractive.

PRACTICE 1

In each of the following sentences, circle the correct form of the verb. Then, write the subject and verb in the blank next to the sentence.

EXAMPLE: *people want*_____ Many people ((want)/wants) to

understand and communicate with whales.

1. _____ In Japan, a professor (believe/believes) that he can talk to a beluga whale.

2. _____ He (say/says) that he uses sound to help a whale understand the meaning of objects and sounds.

3. _____ Whales (communicate/communicates) with each other by using sounds.

4. _____ This whale's name (is/are) Nack.

5. _____ The professor (show/shows) Nack an object and plays a sound.

6. _____ Eventually, the animal (make/makes) the sound when it sees the object.

7. _____ Nack also (choose/chooses) an object when hearing the correct sound.

8. _____ Scientists (want/wants) whales to be able to express their likes and dislikes.

9. _____ However, humans (need/needs) to develop better equipment to hear the sounds that whales make.

10. _____ Researchers (hope/hopes) that whale language will be understood some day.

TIP To do this chapter, you need to understand the following terms: *subject, verb, prepositional phrase, dependent clause,* and *pronoun.* (For review, see Chapters 7 and 8.)

Find and Correct Errors in Subject-Verb Agreement

To find errors in subject-verb agreement, read each sentence in your writing carefully. Make sure that the verb matches the form of the subject. Look for the trouble spots that are detailed later in this chapter.

■ The verb is a form of *be, have,* or *do.*

■ Words or phrases come between the subject and the verb.

- The sentence has a compound subject.
- The subject is an indefinite pronoun.
- The verb comes before the subject.

The Verb Is a Form of *Be, Have,* or *Do*

The verbs *be, have,* and *do* do not follow the regular patterns for forming singular and plural forms; they are **irregular verbs**.

Forms of the Verb *Be* in the Present Tense (Happening Now)

	SINGULAR (ONE ONLY)		PLURAL (TWO OR MORE)	
	If the subject is	. . . then the verb is	If the subject is	. . . then the verb is
First person	I	am	we	are
Second person	you	are	you	are
Third person	he/she/it	is	they	are

Forms of the Verb *Be* in the Past Tense (Happening before Now)

	SINGULAR (ONE ONLY)		PLURAL (TWO OR MORE)	
	If the subject is	. . . then the verb is	If the subject is	. . . then the verb is
First person	I	was	we	were
Second person	you	were	you	were
Third person	he/she/it	was	they	were

INCORRECT

You *is* the fastest driver.

Most books in this library *is* hard.

During the holiday season, the shopping malls *was* busy.

CORRECT

You *are* the fastest driver.
[The second-person singular, *you*, takes *are* as the verb.]

Most books in this library *are* hard.
[The third-person plural, *books*, takes *are* as the verb.]

During the holiday season, the shopping malls *were* busy.
[The third-person plural, *malls*, takes *were* as the verb.]

Forms of the Verb *Have* in the Present Tense (Happening Now)

	SINGULAR (ONE ONLY)		PLURAL (TWO OR MORE)	
	If the subject is	. . . then the verb is	If the subject is	. . . then the verb is
First person	I	have	we	have
Second person	you	have	you	have
Third person	he/she/it	has	they	have

INCORRECT

I *has* the right to see my records.

They *has* the parking permit.

CORRECT

I *have* the right to see my records.
[The first-person singular, *I*, takes *have* as the verb.]

They *have* the parking permit.
[The third-person plural, *they*, takes *have* as the verb.]

Forms of the Verb *Do* in the Present Tense (Happening Now)

	SINGULAR (ONE ONLY)		PLURAL (TWO OR MORE)	
	If the <u>subject</u> is	. . . then the <u>verb</u> is	If the <u>subject</u> is	. . . then the <u>verb</u> is
First person	I	do	we	do
Second person	you	do	you	do
Third person	he/she/it	does	they	do

INCORRECT

<u>She</u> always *do* her assignments on time.

<u>They</u> *does* not like to swim.

CORRECT

<u>She</u> always *does* her assignments on time.
[The third-person singular, *she*, takes *does* as the verb.]

<u>They</u> *do* not like to swim.
[The third-person plural, *they*, takes *do* as the verb.]

PRACTICE 2

In the following paragraph, correct problems with subject-verb agreement.
If a sentence is correct as written, write **C** next to it. There are five correct
sentences.

1 My family have trouble finding time to eat dinner together. **2** We do
our best. **3** Our busy schedules is hard to work around, however. **4** We are
aware of the importance of regular family meals. **5** Scientists has found
interesting benefits to such meals. **6** One study are especially revealing.
7 According to this study, teenagers does less drinking and smoking if
they eat with family members an average of five to seven times weekly.
8 Family mealtime also has a link to eating disorders. **9** A teen girl are less
likely to be anorexic or bulimic if she regularly eats meals with her family.

10 Family dinners even does wonders for children's language development. **11** Mealtime is more important to children's vocabulary than play, story time, and other family activities. **12** Of course, long discussions is more useful for vocabulary skills than comments like "Eat your vegetables." **13** Vegetables is certainly important, too, and children eat more of them when dining with their families. **14** Like most people, you probably has a busy schedule. **15** Nevertheless, family dinners are clearly well worth the time.

Words Come between the Subject and the Verb

TIP For a list of common prepositions, see page 90.

A prepositional phrase or a dependent clause often comes between the subject and the verb. Even when the subject and the verb are not next to each other in the sentence, they still must agree.

A **prepositional phrase** starts with a preposition and ends with a noun or pronoun:

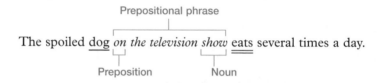

A **dependent clause** has a subject and a verb but does not express a complete thought. When a dependent clause comes between the subject and the verb, it usually starts with the word *who, whose, whom, that,* or *which*.

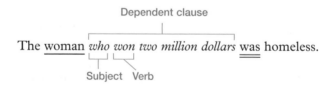

Remember, the subject of a sentence is never in a prepositional phrase or dependent clause.

To find and correct an agreement problem when the subject and the verb are not next to each other, underline the subject, and double-underline the verb in your sentence. Then cross out any words between the subject and verb (a prepositional phrase or dependent clause).

AGREEMENT ERROR   The man ~~who grew those giant tomatoes~~ win at the fair every year.

If the subject is singular (as in the example sentence), the verb must also be singular. If the subject is plural, then the verb must also be plural.

wins

CORRECTED   The man who grew those giant tomatoes ~~win~~ at the
                fair every year.
                                              ^

Read the following sentences, emphasizing the subject and the verb and mentally crossing out the words between them.

INCORRECT

The best <u>deal</u> with the greatest savings <u>*are*</u> at that store.

<u>Items</u> for sale <u>*includes*</u> a baby carriage.

The <u>chef</u> who studied at one of their schools <u>*make*</u> good money.

Some county <u>records</u> that burned in the fire <u>*was*</u> replaced.

CORRECT

The best <u>deal</u> ~~with the greatest savings~~ <u>*is*</u> at that store.

<u>Items</u> ~~for sale~~ <u>*include*</u> a baby carriage.

The <u>chef</u> ~~who studied at one of their schools~~ <u>*makes*</u> good money.

Some county <u>records</u> ~~that burned in the fire~~ <u>*were*</u> replaced.

. . . .

PRACTICE 3

In each sentence of the following paragraph, cross out any prepositional phrases or dependent clauses that come between the subject and the verb. Then, correct all verbs that do not agree with their subjects. Two sentences are correct; write **C** next to them.

1 Visitors to the ruins at Chichen Itza in Mexico is impressed with the ancient Mayan city. **2** A ninety-foot-tall pyramid with steps on each of its four sides stand in the center of the site. **3** This central pyramid, the largest of all Chichen Itza's structures, were built over 1,500 years ago. **4** A temple that was built at the top of the pyramid honors the Mayan god Kukulcan. **5** A throne that was discovered inside the temple in the 1930s are carved in the shape of a jaguar. **6** The Sacred Cenote, where the ancient Mayans made sacrifices to the gods, lie a short distance from the main pyramid. **7** A small road off to the side of the ruins lead to the Sacred Cenote. **8** The Main Ball Court, which has a long narrow playing field, is also located near the temple. **9** Carved images of ball players on the walls next to the ball court was made centuries ago. **10** Archeologists who want to learn more about the Mayan culture continues to study the ruins at Chichen Itza.

. . . .

The Sentence Has a Compound Subject

If two (or more) subjects are joined by *and,* they form a **compound** (plural) **subject,** which requires a plural verb.

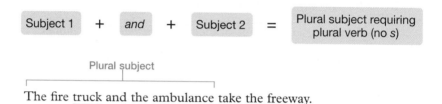

The fire <u>truck</u> and the <u>ambulance</u> <u>take</u> the freeway.

If two (or more) subjects are connected by *or* or *nor,* they are actually considered separate, and the verb agrees with the closer subject.

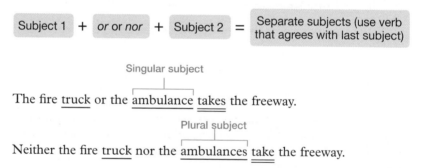

The fire <u>truck</u> or the <u>ambulance</u> <u>takes</u> the freeway.

Neither the fire <u>truck</u> nor the <u>ambulances</u> <u>take</u> the freeway.

To find and correct an agreement problem with compound subjects, underline the subjects, and double-underline the verb in your sentence. Then circle the *and, or,* or *nor* between the subjects.

AGREEMENT   Two <u>soldiers</u> ⓞⓡ an <u>officer</u> always <u>wait</u> at the door.
ERROR

If the circled word is *and* a plural verb is needed. If the circled word is *or* or *nor,* the verb must agree with the subject that is closer to the verb. In the example sentence, *or* separates the subjects, so the verb must agree with *officer* (singular).

CORRECTED   Two soldiers or an officer always ~~wait~~ *waits* at the door.

INCORRECT

The Girl Scouts and their leader *buys* the leftover cookies.

Neither his children nor his dog *like* him.

CORRECT

The Girl Scouts and their leader *buy* the leftover cookies.
[The subject is plural.]

Neither his children nor his dog *likes* him.
[The verb agrees with the closest subject, *dog*.]

PRACTICE 4

In the following paragraph, correct problems with subject-verb agreement. Three sentences are correct; write **C** next to them.

1 Diet and exercise is important parts of a healthy lifestyle. **2** Unfortunately, laziness or bad habits controls the way we eat in many cases. **3** Doctors and nutritionists recommends starting every day with a healthy breakfast. **4** On busy mornings, however, a doughnut or a muffin seem easier than more nutritious options. **5** A healthy lunch or dinner are easier to prepare than many people think. **6** However, frozen food or fast food seems easier than preparing a fresh, healthy meal. **7** As a result, our health and wallets suffer. **8** At a fast-food restaurant, fries and a drink comes in a combination meal. **9** Most children and adults orders the combination meal, even when they want only a hamburger. **10** In many cases, the easiest choice or the most familiar choice is not the best choice for our health.

The Subject Is an Indefinite Pronoun

Indefinite pronouns, which refer to unspecified people or objects, are often singular, although there are exceptions.

Indefinite Pronouns

ALWAYS SINGULAR (USE THE *IS* FORM OF *BE*)		
anybody	everyone	nothing
anyone	everything	one (of)
anything	much	somebody
each (of)	neither (of)	someone
either (of)	nobody	something
everybody	no one	

ALWAYS PLURAL (USE THE *ARE* FORM OF *BE*)	
both	many

MAY BE SINGULAR OR PLURAL (USE THE *IS* OR *ARE* FORM OF *BE*)	
all	none
any	some

Nobody wants to tell him the bad news.

[*Nobody* is always singular, so it takes the singular verb *wants*.]

Some of the soldiers stay on base over the weekend.

[In this case, *some* is plural, referring to some (more than one but less than all) of the *soldiers,* so it takes the plural verb *stay*.]

When you give makeup as a gift, remember that some is hypoallergenic.

[In this case, *some* is singular, so it takes the singular verb *is*.]

Often, an indefinite pronoun is followed by a prepositional phrase or a dependent clause; remember that the subject of a sentence is never found in either of these. To choose the correct verb, you can cross out the prepositional phrase or dependent clause to focus on the indefinite pronoun.

AGREEMENT ERROR   Everyone ~~in this house~~ read the Sunday paper.

Because the subject is singular, the verb must also be singular, so the sentence must be revised.

CORRECTED   Everyone in this house ~~read~~ *reads* the Sunday paper.

INCORRECT

Anyone in the choir *sing* better than I do.

Both of them *is* graduates of this college.

Someone, whom I cannot remember at the moment, always *leave*
early.

Many who buy tickets early *feels* cheated when a concert is canceled.

CORRECT

Anyone ~~in the choir~~ *sings* better than I do.
[The subject is *anyone,* which takes a singular verb.]

Both ~~of them~~ *are* graduates of this college.
[The subject is *both,* which always takes a plural verb.]

Someone, ~~whom I cannot remember at the moment,~~ always *leaves*
early.
[*Someone* is always singular.]

Many ~~who buy tickets early~~ *feel* cheated when a concert is canceled.
[The subject is *many,* which is always plural.]

. . . .

PRACTICE 5

In each of the following sentences, circle the verb that agrees with the subject.

    EXAMPLE: One of my daughters (wants)/ want) her own pet.

1. Everyone (thinks / think) that this is a good chance to teach her
responsibility.

2. No one (knows / know) why, but she is not interested in puppies and
kittens.

3. Someone in her class (owns / own) a goldfish and some Sea Monkeys.

4. Either (makes / make) a good first pet.

5. Everybody who has raised Sea Monkeys (tells / tell) me that they are
inexpensive and easy to care for.

6. One of my daughter's friends (thinks / think) that the small creatures
are related to monkeys.

7. Neither of my children (believes/believe) this.

8. Each of the tiny animals (is/are) actually a type of shrimp.

9. Everybody (loves/love) to watch the little shrimp wiggle around in the water.

10. Everyone who (enjoys/enjoy) Sea Monkeys can thank Harold von Braunhut, who started selling the shrimp eggs in 1957.

The Verb Comes before the Subject

In most sentences, the subject comes before the verb. However, the verb comes *before* the subject in questions and in sentences that begin with *here* or *there*. To find the subject and verb, turn these sentences around.

Which is the prize that you won? The prize that you won is . . .

Where are the envelopes? The envelopes are . . .

Notice that turning a question around means answering it.

Here is the magazine that I promised to bring you. The magazine that I promised to bring you is here.

There are several pictures on the wall. Several pictures are on the wall.

Check your writing for questions and sentences that begin with *here* or *there*.

AGREEMENT ERRORS   Where is the carpenter's tools?

Here is the carpenter's tools.

To see if there is an error, turn the sentences around. Underline the subjects, and double-underline the verbs.

AGREEMENT ERRORS   The carpenter's tools is where?

The carpenter's tools is here.

If the subject is singular, it needs to have a singular verb, and if it is plural, it needs to have a plural verb. In the example sentences, the subject is plural, but the verb (*is*) is singular.

CORRECTED   Where ~~is~~ *are* the carpenter's tools?

Here ~~is~~ *are* the carpenter's tools.

INCORRECT

There *is* the paintbrushes I brought you.

CORRECT

There *are* the paintbrushes I brought you.

[The paintbrushes *are* there.]

PRACTICE 6

In the following paragraph, correct problems with subject-verb agreement. Three sentences are correct; write **C** next to them.

1 Here are the farm stand we were telling you about. **2** It sells the freshest fruits and vegetables that you will ever taste. **3** The corn is picked fresh every morning. **4** Where is the fields in which it is grown? **5** Here is tomatoes loaded with flavor. **6** Is the watermelons in that box too big for one person to carry? **7** Here are homemade ice cream fresh from the freezer. **8** Where are the prize-winning cherry pies? **9** There are an apple pie that is still steaming from the oven. **10** There are no space in the car for all that I want to eat.

PRACTICE 7

In the following passage, correct problems with subject-verb agreement. Four sentences are correct; write **C** next to them. The first sentence has been edited for you.

1 Members of a law enforcement agency collects evidence before making an arrest. **2** There is three main types of evidence: testimonial, documentary, and physical evidence. **3** Someone who has firsthand knowledge of a crime provide testimonial evidence. **4** As its name suggests, documentary evidence consists of written documents as well as audio and video recordings. **5** Physical evidence, in contrast, is an object or a material that might link a suspect to the scene of a crime. **6** Fingerprints and DNA is physical evidence. **7** Other examples of physical evidence includes drugs, weapons, and fibers from clothing. **8** Generally, testimonial evidence and documentary evidence are not as reliable as physical evidence.

    9 The Fourth Amendment of the U.S. Constitution regulate the collection of evidence. **10** To obtain a search warrant, a law-enforcement officer have to give a good reason, or probable cause. **11** However, a search warrant is not always required. **12** For example, an officer do not need a warrant to search for marijuana fields by helicopter. **13** In certain situations, an officer have the authority to search a car without a warrant. **14** There is many citizens who disagree with such exceptions. **15** Neither security nor freedom are worth sacrificing for the other, they believe.

12

Verb-Tense Problems

The Past Tense and the Past Participle

Understand Regular Verbs in the Past Tense

Verb tense tells *when* the action of a sentence occurs. The **past tense** describes actions that began and ended in the past. To form the past tense of most **regular verbs**, add *-ed*. For verbs that end in *e*, just add a *-d*.

TIP To do this chapter, you may want to review Chapters 7 and 8.

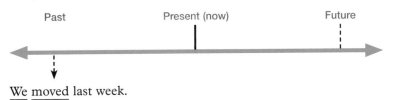

We <u>moved</u> last week.

Regular Verbs in the Past Tense

PRESENT / PAST		
Regular verbs → add -ed	**Regular verbs ending with -e → add -d**	**Regular verbs ending with -y → change -y to -i and add -ed**
learn / learn**ed**	move / move**d**	worry / worr**ied**
pass / pass**ed**	smoke / smoke**d**	cry / cr**ied**
finish / finish**ed**	hire / hire**d**	try / tr**ied**
start / start**ed**	stare / stare**d**	hurry / hurr**ied**
work / work**ed**	rescue / rescue**d**	party / part**ied**
play / play**ed**	excuse / excuse**d**	study / stud**ied**

TIP Consonants are *b, c, d, f, g, h, j, k, l, m, n, p, q, r, s, t, v, w, x, z,* and sometimes *y.*

✓ LearningCurve For extra practice in the skills covered in this chapter, visit
bedfordstmartins.com/rsinteractive.

PRACTICE 1

In the following paragraph, fill in the correct past-tense form of each verb in parentheses.

   1 Two months ago, workers _____ (install) a new alarm system in my dormitory. **2** We _____ (use) to be able to leave the door ajar for guests, but not anymore. **3** Last weekend, my roommate _____ (call) me at three o'clock in the morning to tell me she could not get in. **4** We _____ (complain) to campus security that the new system is inconvenient. **5** They _____ (appreciate) our concerns, but they _____ (remind) us that there were four thefts in our building last semester. **6** Parents and students _____ (worry) that something even more serious could happen without better security. **7** The students and staff _____ (decide) together that something _____ (need) to be done. **8** After they _____ (research) several systems, campus security chose the alarm system that automatically _____ (connect) to the police station after thirty seconds. **9** Representatives from the alarm company _____ (train) the staff on the new system and _____ (warn) them that the police will start fining us if we set off too many false alarms. **10** The alarm company _____ (estimate) that we will have no break-ins at our dorm this semester, and so far they are right.

Understand Irregular Verbs in the Past Tense

Irregular verbs do not follow the regular pattern of adding *-d* or *-ed* for the past tense. Practice using these verbs.

Irregular Verbs in the Past Tense

BASE VERB	PAST TENSE	BASE VERB	PAST TENSE
be (am/are/is)	was/were	bite	bit
become	became	blow	blew
begin	began	break	broke

BASE VERB	PAST TENSE
bring	brought
build	built
buy	bought
catch	caught
choose	chose
come	came
cost	cost
dive	dived/dove
do	did
draw	drew
drink	drank
drive	drove
eat	ate
fall	fell
feed	fed
feel	felt
fight	fought
find	found
fly	flew
forget	forgot
freeze	froze
get	got
give	gave
go	went
grow	grew
have/has	had
hear	heard
hide	hid
hit	hit
hold	held
hurt	hurt

BASE VERB	PAST TENSE
get	got
give	gave
go	went
grow	grew
have/has	had
hear	heard
hide	hid
hit	hit
hold	held
hurt	hurt
keep	kept
know	knew
lay	laid
lead	led
leave	left
let	let
lie	lay
light	lit
lose	lost
make	made
mean	meant
meet	met
pay	paid
put	put
quit	quit
read	read
ride	rode
ring	rang
rise	rose
run	ran

BASE VERB	PAST TENSE	BASE VERB	PAST TENSE
say	said	sting	stung
see	saw	strike	struck
sell	sold	swim	swam
send	sent		
shake	shook	take	took
show	showed	teach	taught
shrink	shrank	tear	tore
shut	shut	tell	told
sing	sang	think	thought
sink	sank	throw	threw
sit	sat		
sleep	slept	understand	understood
speak	spoke		
spend	spent	wake	woke
stand	stood	wear	wore
steal	stole	win	won
stick	stuck	write	wrote

PRACTICE 2

In each sentence of the following paragraph, fill in the correct past-tense forms of the irregular verbs in parentheses.

1 After high school, I _____ (think) college would get in the way of all my fun. 2 I _____ (spend) most of my time working and partying, and no time thinking about college or my future. 3 I worked as a waitress and _____ (make) enough money to pay my bills. 4 After three years of waitressing, however, I _____ (feel) that I was accomplishing nothing. 5 That is when I _____ (begin) taking classes at our local college. 6 I _____ (take) three classes that first semester, in reading, math, and English. 7 Although it was hard to get back into the routine of going to class and doing homework, I _____ (stick) with it. 8 I gradually _____ (become) better at managing my workload and still finding some free time to have fun. 9 By the time finals _____

(come) at the end of the year, I was nervous but ready. **10** I _____
(get) two A's and a B that first semester back at college, and I was glad to
know that all my hard work had paid off.

Understand Four Very Irregular Verbs

Some irregular verbs cause confusion and require special attention: *be, have,
can,* and *will.*

The Verb *Be*

Be is tricky because its singular and plural forms are different, in both present and past tenses.

TIP *Be* is used with the past participle to form the passive voice, covered on page 150.

Present- and Past-Tense Forms of *Be*

	SINGULAR		PLURAL	
	Present →	Past tense	Present →	Past tense
First person	I am →	I was	we are →	we were
Second person	you are →	you were	you are →	you were
Third person	he/she/it is →	he/she/it was	they are →	they were

---

PRACTICE 3

In the following paragraph, fill in each blank with the correct past-tense form of *be*.

　　1 When our electricity bill for last month arrived, we _____
surprised. **2** The bill _____ for $3,218. **3** I _____
sure that this impossibly high amount _____ wrong. **4** Right
away, my roommate and I _____ on the phone with the electric
company. **5** The representatives with whom we spoke _____
of no help. **6** Each of them said that we _____ wrong and
had to pay the bill. **7** A friend of mine who works for a cable company

TIP In the chart above, and in later charts and sentence examples, subjects are underlined and verbs are double-underlined.

_____ much more helpful. **8** She _____ eager to give us advice. **9** If we continued complaining politely and regularly, she _____ sure that the company would correct the bill. **10** After a month of polite complaints and letters, we _____ pleased to receive a corrected bill of $218, which we immediately paid.

The Verb *Have*

Present- and Past-Tense Forms of *Have*

	SINGULAR		PLURAL	
	Present →	Past tense	Present →	Past tense
First person	I have →	I had	we have →	we had
Second person	you have →	you had	you have →	you had
Third person	he/she/it has →	he/she/it had	they have →	they had

PRACTICE 4

TIP *Have* is used with the past participle, covered on pages 140, 146–149, and 156–158.

In each of the following sentences, circle the correct form of *have:* present or past tense.

EXAMPLE: More than 90 percent of the people in the United States (have / had) a cell phone today.

1. Unfortunately, according to several different studies, a cell phone (has / had) a number of risks associated with it.

2. First of all, many drivers (have / had) their attention on their phones and not on the road.

3. Statistics (have / had) shown that drivers who talk on the phone run a much higher risk of having an accident than drivers who do not use phones.

4. Other concerns about cell phone use (have / had) some researchers worried.

5. Radiation is emitted from these phones, and doctors (have / had) evidence that these emissions can be harmful to humans.

. . . .

Can / Could and Will / Would

People mix up the past- and present-tense forms of these tricky verbs. The verb *can* means *able*. Its past-tense form is *could*. The verb *will* expresses a plan. Its past-tense form is *would*.

PRESENT TENSE   He can play poker daily. [He is able to play poker daily.]

He will play poker daily. [He plans to play poker daily.]

PAST TENSE   He could play poker daily. [He was able to play poker daily.]

He would play poker daily. [He planned to play (and did play) poker daily.]

In these examples, *can, could, will,* and *would* are helping verbs followed by the main verb *play*. Notice that the main verb is in the base form (*play*). It does not change from present to past.

Present- and Past-Tense Forms of *Can* and *Will*

	CAN / COULD		WILL / WOULD	
	Present	Past tense	Present	Past tense
First person	I / we can	I / we could	I / we will	I / we would
Second person	you can	you could	you will	you would
Third person	he / she / it can they can	he / she / it could they could	he / she / it will they will	he / she / it would they would

PRACTICE 5

In each of the following sentences, circle the correct verb.

> **EXAMPLE:** This morning, Dane said that he (can /(could)) teach
>
> himself how to use our new digital camera.

1. Several hours and many fuzzy pictures later, he admitted that he (can / could) not figure out how to use the camera's fancy features.

2. I decided that I (will / would) help him.

3. Next week, it (will / would) not be my fault if our vacation photographs turn out fuzzy.

4. After reading the manual myself, I showed him how he (can / could) take better pictures.

5. Now he (can / could) use the camera like a professional.

Understand the Past Participle

The **past participle** is a verb form that is used with a helping verb, such as *has* or *have*.

Helping verb   Past participle

Bees have swarmed around the hive all summer.

Past Participles of Regular Verbs

To form the past participle of a regular verb, add *-d* or *-ed*. For regular verbs, the past-participle form looks just like the past tense.

TIP To do this chapter, you may want to review the terms *subject, verb,* and *helping verb* from Chapters 7 and 8.

Regular Verbs and Their Past Participles

BASE FORM	PAST TENSE	PAST PARTICIPLE
(Usually I . . .)	(Yesterday I . . .)	(Over time, I have . . .)
collect	collected	collected
dine	dined	dined
talk	talked	talked

PRACTICE 6

In each of the following sentences, underline the helping verb *has* or *have,* and fill in the correct past-participle form of the verb in parentheses.

> **EXAMPLE:** The Internet has _____*attracted*_____ (attract) millions of
>
> users, many of them young people.

1. Internet safety rules have _____ (help) to remind children and young adults of potential dangers.

2. One of these safety rules has _____ (center) on not revealing any personal information, such as name, address, telephone number, or Social Security number.

3. Parents have _____ (remind) their children to treat others respectfully when online but not to be too trusting.

4. Many parents have _____ (decide) to allow their children to visit approved Web sites and to block access to dangerous sites.

5. A responsible parent has _____ (discuss) with his or her child the need to be cautious when meeting people online.

Past Participles of Irregular Verbs

The past participles of irregular verbs do not match their past-tense form, and they do not follow a regular pattern.

Irregular Verbs and Their Past Participles

BASE FORM	PAST TENSE	PAST PARTICIPLE
(Usually I . . .)	*(Yesterday I . . .)*	*(Over time, I have . . .)*
drive	drove	driven
see	saw	seen
throw	threw	thrown

Irregular Verbs and Their Past Participles

BASE VERB	PAST TENSE	PAST PARTICIPLE
be (am / are / is)	was / were	been
become	became	become
begin	began	begun
bite	bit	bitten
blow	blew	blown
break	broke	broken
bring	brought	brought
build	built	built
buy	bought	bought
catch	caught	caught
choose	chose	chosen
come	came	come
cost	cost	cost
dive	dived / dove	dived
do	did	done
draw	drew	drawn
drink	drank	drunk
drive	drove	driven
eat	ate	eaten
fall	fell	fallen
feed	fed	fed
feel	felt	felt
fight	fought	fought
find	found	found
fly	flew	flown
forget	forgot	forgotten
freeze	froze	frozen
get	got	gotten
give	gave	given

BASE VERB	PAST TENSE	PAST PARTICIPLE
go	went	gone
grow	grew	grown
have/has	had	had
hear	heard	heard
hide	hid	hidden
hit	hit	hit
hold	held	held
hurt	hurt	hurt
keep	kept	kept
know	knew	known
lay	laid	laid
lead	led	led
leave	left	left
let	let	let
lie	lay	lain
light	lit	lit
lose	lost	lost
make	made	made
mean	meant	meant
meet	met	met
pay	paid	paid
put	put	put
quit	quit	quit
read	read	read
ride	rode	ridden
ring	rang	rung
rise	rose	risen
run	ran	run

BASE VERB	PAST TENSE	PAST PARTICIPLE
say	said	said
see	saw	seen
sell	sold	sold
send	sent	sent
shake	shook	shaken
show	showed	shown
shrink	shrank	shrunk
shut	shut	shut
sing	sang	sung
sink	sank	sunk
sit	sat	sat
sleep	slept	slept
speak	spoke	spoken
spend	spent	spent
stand	stood	stood
steal	stole	stolen
stick	stuck	stuck
sting	stung	stung
strike	struck	struck, stricken
swim	swam	swum
take	took	taken
teach	taught	taught
tear	tore	torn
tell	told	told
think	thought	thought
throw	threw	thrown
understand	understood	understood
wake	woke	woken
wear	wore	worn
win	won	won
write	wrote	written

. . . .

PRACTICE 7

Edit each of the following sentences to use the helping verb *has* or *have* plus the past-participle form of the verb.

> *have*
> **EXAMPLE:** For many years, people paid their bills by mail.
>   ^

1. Some forgot to pay them on time.

2. Many banks saw people's forgetfulness and tardiness as an opportunity.

3. They gave their customers a new service called online bill pay.

4. It was a great success.

5. Many customers chose this new option.

6. They began paying all their monthly bills online.

7. It became a much easier process for everyone involved.

8. Most customers spoke highly of this service.

9. It took only a short while for people to learn this new way to pay their bills.

10. They wrote checks in the past, but today, all they have to do is click a button.

. . . .

Use the Past Participle Correctly

The **past participle** is used in both the present-perfect and past-perfect tenses. It is also used to form the passive voice.

Present-Perfect Tense

Use the **present perfect** to show two different kinds of actions:

1. An action that started in the past and is still going on:

    The families have vacationed together for years.

2. An action that has just happened or was completed at some
    unspecified time in the past.

The package has arrived.

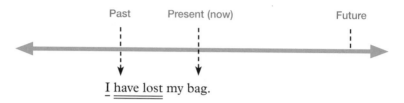

I have lost my bag.

Form the present-perfect tense as follows:

Subject + has/have + Past participle = Present-perfect tense

Note the difference in meaning between the past tense and present-perfect
tense.

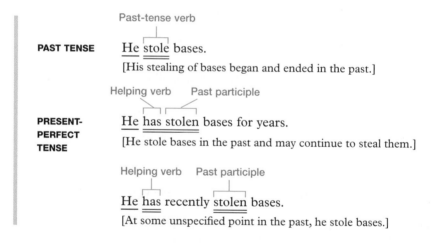

	SINGULAR	PLURAL
First person	I have finished	we have finished
Second person	you have finished	you have finished
Third person	he/she/it has finished	they have finished

INCORRECT

Since 2009, he _traveled_ to five continents.

We worked together for three years now.

Antiwar protests _became_ common in recent years.

CORRECT

Since 2009, he _has traveled_ to five continents.
[He completed his traveling at some unspecified point in the past.]

We _have worked_ together for three years now.
[They still work together.]

Antiwar protests _have become_ common in recent years.
[They continue to be common.]

- -

PRACTICE 8

In the following paragraph, fill in each blank with the correct tense—past or present perfect—of the verb in parentheses.

1 Before there were health clubs, people rarely _____
(have) problems getting along with one another during workouts. **2** Back
then, in fact, most people _____ (work) out by themselves.
3 Today, health clubs and gyms _____ (become) popular
places to exercise. **4** In these physically stressful settings, some people
_____ (forget) how to be polite to others. **5** When we were
young, we all _____ (learn) to take turns when playing with
other children. **6** Our parents _____ (tell) us to treat others
as we would like to be treated ourselves. **7** But in health clubs, some people
_____ (complain) about customers who refuse to share the
equipment. **8** Gym employees say that they _____ (notice)
an increase in the number of arguments between members. **9** Yesterday, I
_____ (see) one woman push another woman off a treadmill.
10 To create a more pleasant atmosphere, some gyms _____
(post) rules and suggestions for their customers. **11** Most people always
_____ (consider) it to be common courtesy to clean up after
themselves. **12** Now, health clubs _____ (begin) to require

that exercisers wipe up any perspiration that they leave on equipment.
13 It seems that the need to stay in shape _____ (create)
mental as well as physical stress for some people. **14** However, it is
important to always keep in mind the basic rules of polite behavior that
our parents _____ (teach) us when we were young.

Past-Perfect Tense

Use the **past-perfect tense** to show an action that was started and completed in the past before another action in the past.

Past	Past	Present (now)	Future

Kara <u>had eaten</u> before she went to class.

Form the past-perfect tense as follows:

Subject + had + Past participle = Past-perfect tense

TIP For a verb reference chart on the perfect tenses, see pages 156–58.

Note the difference in meaning between the past tense and past-perfect tense.

PAST TENSE

Past-tense verb

In March 1954, runner <u>Roger Bannister broke</u> the four-minute mile record.

[One action (breaking the four-minute mile) occurred in the past.]

PAST-PERFECT TENSE

Helping verb   Past participle

Within a month, <u>John Landy had broken</u> Bannister's record.

[Two actions (Bannister's and Landy's races) occurred in the past, but Bannister's action was completed before Landy's action started.]

Past-Perfect Tense (*had* + past participle)

	SINGULAR	PLURAL
First person	I had driven	we had driven
Second person	you had driven	you had driven
Third person	he/she/it had driven	they had driven

PRACTICE 9

In each of the following sentences, circle the correct verb tense.

EXAMPLE: Before we left for our camping trip, we (talked / had talked) about the wildlife at Moosehead Mountain.

1. I decided not to mention the rattlesnake that (scared / had scared) me on last year's trip.

2. I never (was / had been) afraid of snakes until I came that close to one.

3. On this year's trip, we (saw / had seen) something even more frightening than a snake.

4. As my friends and I (planned / had planned), we took a long hike after setting up our tent.

5. By the time we returned to the campsite, the sun (went / had gone) down.

6. Near the tent, we (heard / had heard) a low growl.

7. Suddenly, we (saw / had seen) a dark shadow running into the woods.

8. We realized that a bear (visited / had visited) our campsite.

9. Frightened but tired, we (tried / had tried) to get some rest.

10. When the sun finally came up, we saw that the bear (stayed / had stayed) away, but we (got / had gotten) little sleep.

Passive versus Active Voice

In sentences that use the **passive voice**, the subject is acted on: It receives the action of the verb. The passive voice is formed as follows:

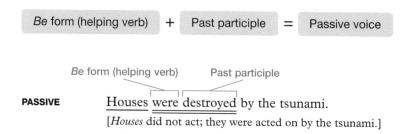

| *Be* form (helping verb) | + | Past participle | = | Passive voice |

PASSIVE   Houses were destroyed by the tsunami.

[*Houses* did not act; they were acted on by the tsunami.]

In sentences that use the **active voice**, the subject performs the action.

ACTIVE   The tsunami destroyed the houses.

Whenever possible, use the active voice. Use the passive voice only when you do not know the specific performer of an action or when you want to emphasize the receiver of the action.

EXAMPLES OF THE CORRECT USE OF ACTIVE AND PASSIVE VOICE

ACTIVE   After the fight, the police took him away.

[We know that the police took him away.]

PASSIVE   After the fight, he was taken away.

[We do not know who took him away.]

PASSIVE   The old bridge was demolished this morning by engineers.

[The important point is that the bridge was demolished.]

PASSIVE   The chemical elements are arranged by their atomic weights.

[Scientific and technical reports frequently use the passive since the focus is often on the idea or thing being acted upon.]

. . . .

PRACTICE 10

In each of the following sentences, underline the verb. In the blank space provided, write **A** if the sentence is in the active voice or **P** if the sentence is in the passive voice.

> **EXAMPLE:** __A__ Many parents assume that their children will stop
>
> eating when they are full.

1. ___ Scientists recently studied this assumption.

2. ___ In the study, children were given more food than necessary.

3. ___ The children almost always ate all the food on their plates.

4. ___ Their level of hunger made no difference.

5. ___ In another study, similar conclusions were drawn.

6. ___ Parents and their children were observed during a typical meal.

7. ___ The parents of overweight children served much larger portions.

8. ___ Often, the overweight children were told to finish everything on their plates.

9. ___ Healthier children were given much smaller amounts of food.

10. ___ The children who served themselves ate the most appropriate amount of food.

. . . .

PRACTICE 11

In the following paragraphs, correct problems with the use of past tense, past participles in the present-perfect and past-perfect tenses, and passive voice.

    1 Few scientific theories have create as much controversy as the theory of evolution. **2** In 1860, Charles Darwin write *The Origin of Species*. **3** The book presented evidence that Darwin has collected on a five-year voyage along the coast of South America. **4** Darwin argued that life on earth begun slowly and gradually. **5** He believe that each species of animals, including humans, has developed from previous species. **6** This theory will have important effects on the study of biology, but it goed against the Bible's account of creation.

    7 Ever since Darwin's theory became knowed, people had been divided on whether evolution should be taught in public schools. **8** Some parents worryed that their children will get confused or upset by these teachings. **9** The first court trial on evolution is in 1925. **10** Earlier, in the small town of Dayton, Tennessee, a biology teacher named John T. Scopes assigned a textbook that described the theory of evolution. **11** The book said that humans had came from earlier forms of life. **12** Earlier that year, the state's Butler Law has banned the teaching of evolution, so Scopes was arrested. **13** Although Scopes's lawyer maked an impressive case against the constitutionality of the Butler Law, Scopes were found guilty, and the law remained intact. **14** In 1967, the Butler Law was ruled unconstitutional by the U.S. Supreme Court. **15** However, recent court cases in Kansas, Ohio, and Pennsylvania have showed that the teaching of evolution in public schools was still a controversial issue. **16** Ever since the Scopes trial, people fought over the issue in courtrooms across the country.

Verb-Tense Reference Chart

THE SIMPLE TENSES

TENSE

Simple Present

TIMELINE: Use in situations that exist always (now, in the past, and in the future).

Past | Present (now) | Future

I like pizza.

STATEMENTS
In the third-person singular, regular verbs end in -s or -es. (For past-tense forms of irregular verbs, see pages 134–36.)

I/you **like** pizza.

We **like** pizza.

She/he **likes** pizza.

They **like** pizza.

NEGATIVES

Present of *do (does)* + *not* + Base verb

I/you **do not like** pizza.

We **do not like** pizza.

She/he **does not like** pizza.

They **do not like** pizza.

QUESTIONS

Present of *do (does)* + Subject + Base verb

Do I/you **like** pizza?

Do we **like** pizza?

Does she/he **like** pizza?

Do they **like** pizza?

TENSE	
Simple Past	**STATEMENTS**

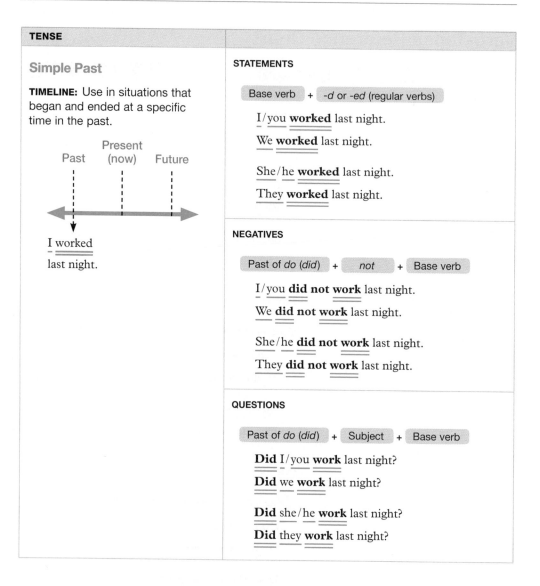

Simple Past

TIMELINE: Use in situations that began and ended at a specific time in the past.

Past   Present (now)   Future

I worked
last night.

STATEMENTS

Base verb + -d or -ed (regular verbs)

I/you **worked** last night.

We **worked** last night.

She/he **worked** last night.

They **worked** last night.

NEGATIVES

Past of *do* (*did*) + *not* + Base verb

I/you **did not work** last night.

We **did not work** last night.

She/he **did not work** last night.

They **did not work** last night.

QUESTIONS

Past of *do* (*did*) + Subject + Base verb

Did I/you **work** last night?

Did we **work** last night?

Did she/he **work** last night?

Did they **work** last night?

TENSE	
Simple Future **TIMELINE:** Use in situations that will begin in the future. 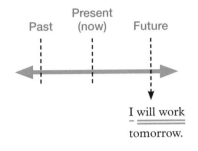 I will work tomorrow.	**STATEMENTS** Will + Base verb Maybe I/you **will work** tomorrow. Maybe she/he/it **will work** tomorrow. Maybe we/you/they **will work** tomorrow. **NEGATIVES** Will + not + Base verb Maybe I/you **will not work** tomorrow. **QUESTIONS** Will + Subject + Base verb **Will** I/you **work** tomorrow?

THE PERFECT TENSES

TENSE	

Present Perfect

TIMELINE: Use in a situation that began in the past and either is still happening or ended at an unknown time in the past.

Past   Present (now)   Future

I have attended every class.

STATEMENTS

Present of *have* + Past participle of base verb

I/you **have attended** every class.

She/he **has attended** every class.

We **have attended** every class.

They **have attended** every class.

NEGATIVES

Present of *have* + *not* + Past participle of base verb

I/you **have not attended** every class.

She/he **has not attended** every class.

We **have not attended** every class.

They **have not attended** every class.

QUESTIONS

Present of *have* + Subject + Past participle of base verb

Have I/you **attended** every class?

Has she/he **attended** every class?

Have we **attended** every class?

Have they **attended** every class?

TENSE	

Past Perfect

TIMELINE: Use in a situation that began and ended before some other past situation occurred.

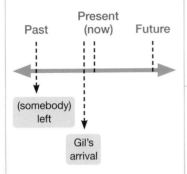

STATEMENTS

Past of *have (had)* + Past participle of base verb

I/you **had left** before Gil arrived.

She/he **had left** before **Gil arrived**.

We **had left** before **Gil arrived**.

They **had left** before **Gil arrived**.

NEGATIVES

Past of *have (had)* + *not* + Past participle of base verb

Usually used for "if" situations

If you **had not left**, you would have seen him.

If she/he **had not left**, she/he would have seen him.

If we **had not left**, we would have seen him.

If they **had not left**, they would have seen him.

QUESTIONS

Past of *have (had)* + Subject + Past participle of base verb

Had I/you **left** before Gil arrived?

Had she/he **left** before Gil arrived?

Had we **left** before Gil arrived?

Had they **left** before Gil arrived?

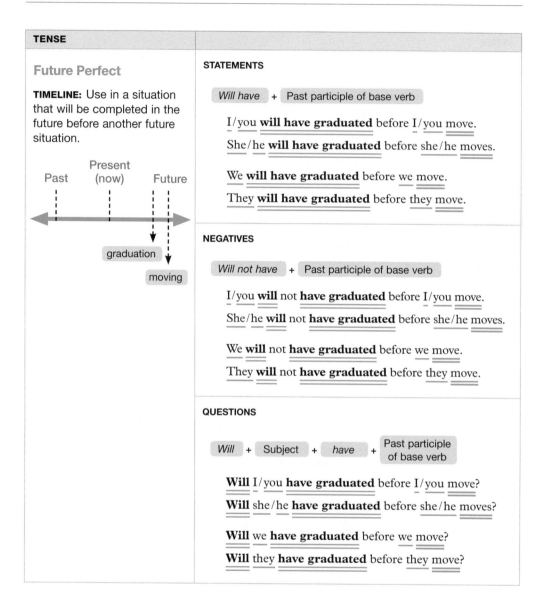

TENSE	
Future Perfect	**STATEMENTS**

Future Perfect

TIMELINE: Use in a situation that will be completed in the future before another future situation.

Past — Present (now) — Future

graduation
moving

STATEMENTS

Will have + Past participle of base verb

I/you **will have graduated** before I/you move.

She/he **will have graduated** before she/he moves.

We **will have graduated** before we move.

They **will have graduated** before they move.

NEGATIVES

Will not have + Past participle of base verb

I/you **will** not **have graduated** before I/you move.

She/he **will** not **have graduated** before she/he moves.

We **will** not **have graduated** before we move.

They **will** not **have graduated** before they move.

QUESTIONS

Will + Subject + have + Past participle of base verb

Will I/you **have graduated** before I/you move?

Will she/he **have graduated** before she/he moves?

Will we **have graduated** before we move?

Will they **have graduated** before they move?

THE PROGRESSIVE TENSES

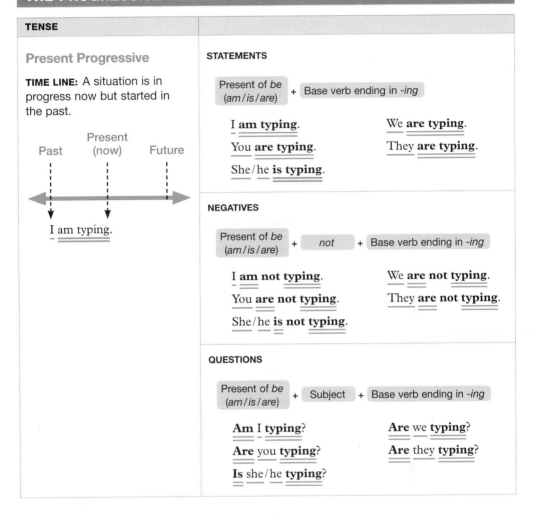

TENSE	
Present Progressive	**STATEMENTS**

TIME LINE: A situation is in progress now but started in the past.

Past / Present (now) / Future

I am typing.

STATEMENTS

Present of *be* (am/is/are) + Base verb ending in *-ing*

I **am typing**.   We **are typing**.
You **are typing**.   They **are typing**.
She/he **is typing**.

NEGATIVES

Present of *be* (am/is/are) + *not* + Base verb ending in *-ing*

I **am not typing**.   We **are not typing**.
You **are not typing**.   They **are not typing**.
She/he **is not typing**.

QUESTIONS

Present of *be* (am/is/are) + Subject + Base verb ending in *-ing*

Am I **typing**?   **Are** we **typing**?
Are you **typing**?   **Are** they **typing**?
Is she/he **typing**?

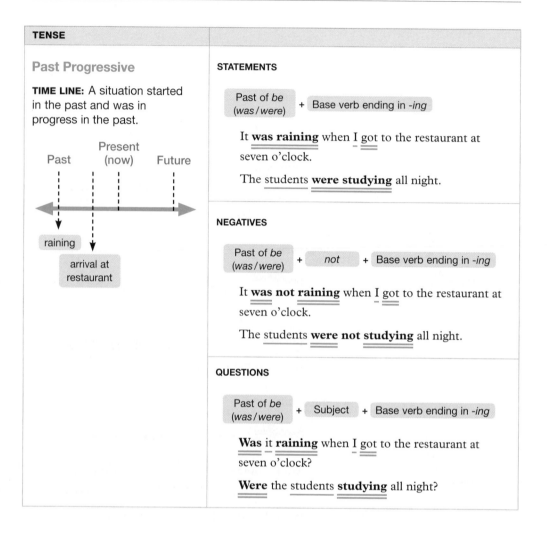

TENSE	
Past Progressive	**STATEMENTS**

Past Progressive

TIME LINE: A situation started in the past and was in progress in the past.

STATEMENTS

Past of *be* (*was/were*) + Base verb ending in *-ing*

It **was raining** when I got to the restaurant at seven o'clock.

The students **were studying** all night.

NEGATIVES

Past of *be* (*was/were*) + *not* + Base verb ending in *-ing*

It **was not raining** when I got to the restaurant at seven o'clock.

The students **were not studying** all night.

QUESTIONS

Past of *be* (*was/were*) + Subject + Base verb ending in *-ing*

Was it **raining** when I got to the restaurant at seven o'clock?

Were the students **studying** all night?

TENSE	
Future Progressive	**STATEMENTS**

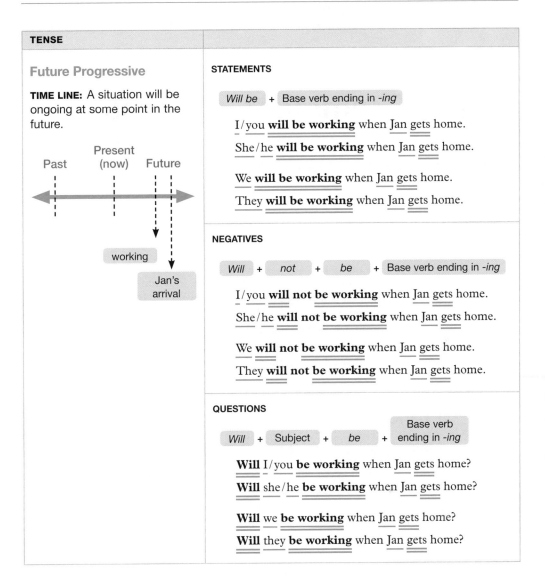

Future Progressive

TIME LINE: A situation will be ongoing at some point in the future.

STATEMENTS

Will be + Base verb ending in *-ing*

I/you **will be working** when Jan gets home.

She/he **will be working** when Jan gets home.

We **will be working** when Jan gets home.

They **will be working** when Jan gets home.

NEGATIVES

Will + *not* + *be* + Base verb ending in *-ing*

I/you **will not be working** when Jan gets home.

She/he **will not be working** when Jan gets home.

We **will not be working** when Jan gets home.

They **will not be working** when Jan gets home.

QUESTIONS

Will + Subject + *be* + Base verb ending in *-ing*

Will I/you **be working** when Jan gets home?

Will she/he **be working** when Jan gets home?

Will we **be working** when Jan gets home?

Will they **be working** when Jan gets home?

13

Other Grammar Concerns

Problems with Pronouns and Modifiers

In addition to checking your writing for the four most serious errors covered in Chapters 9 through 12, you will want to be aware of common trouble spots with pronouns, adjectives and adverbs, and misplaced and dangling modifiers. Style issues (choppy sentences and paralellism) and word usage are covered in Chapter 14; matters of punctuation and capitalization are addressed in Chapter 15.

Pronouns

Make Pronouns Agree with Their Antecedents

A pronoun must agree with (match) the noun or pronoun that it refers to in number: Both must be singular (one) or plural (more than one).

The Riccis opened *their* new store yesterday.

[*Their* agrees with *Riccis* because both are plural.]

TIP For a review of pronouns, see pages 82–86.

If a pronoun refers to a singular noun, it must also match that noun in gender: *he* for masculine nouns, *she* for feminine nouns, and *it* for genderless nouns. Do not use *their,* a plural pronoun, when the noun that it replaces is singular. To avoid this common pronoun error, use a singular pronoun for a singular noun or make the noun plural.

INCORRECT   A new student must get *their* college identification card.

[*Student* is singular; the pronoun that refers to *student* (*their*) is plural.]

LearningCurve **For extra practice in the skills covered in this chapter, visit**
bedfordstmartins.com/rsinteractive.

CORRECT	A new student must get *his or her* college identification card.
	[*Student* and *his or her* are singular.]
CORRECT	New *students* must get *their* college identification cards.
	[Both *students* and *their* are plural.]

Although using a masculine pronoun alone (*A new student must get* his *college identification card*) is grammatically correct, it is considered sexist language. Avoid it.

Two types of words often cause errors in pronoun agreement: indefinite pronouns and collective nouns.

INDEFINITE PRONOUNS

An **indefinite pronoun** does not refer to a specific person, place, thing, or idea. Indefinite pronouns often take singular verbs.

Indefinite Pronouns

ALWAYS SINGULAR

another	everyone	nothing
anybody	everything	one (of)
anyone	much	somebody
anything	neither (of)	someone
each (of)	nobody	something
either (of)	no one	
everybody		

ALWAYS PLURAL

both	many
few	several

MAY BE SINGULAR OR PLURAL

all	none
any	some
most	

When you see or write a sentence that has an indefinite pronoun, choose the word that goes with this pronoun carefully.

INCORRECT

The priests assembled in the hall. Each had *their* own seat.

Almost no one likes to hear a recording of *their* voice.

CORRECT

The priests assembled in the hall. Each had *his* own seat.

[The singular pronoun *his* matches the singular pronoun *each*.]

Almost no one likes to hear a recording of *his or her* voice.

[The singular pronouns *his or her* match the singular pronoun *no one*.]

In some cases, indefinite nouns are plural. (Check the chart on p. 163 to see which ones are always plural.)

INCORRECT

Several professional athletes admit that *he or she* has used performance-enhancing drugs.

CORRECT

Several professional athletes admit that *they* have used performance-enhancing drugs.

· ·

PRACTICE 1

Circle the correct pronoun or group of words in parentheses.

1 Anyone who goes to a seminar thinking that (he or she / they) can ignore high-pressure sales tactics for a free gift is probably mistaken. **2** Each of these types of sales representatives has perfected (his or her / their) sales pitch to guarantee some success. **3** Few people can resist the promise of a free gift in exchange for a small amount of (his or her / their) time. **4** The pitch begins in a friendly and comfortable setting, usually with refreshments, where nobody would feel that (he or she / they) might get taken advantage of. **5** Everyone at the seminar is assigned (his or her / their) own personal "consultant" to find out which product — such as real estate, insurance, financial investments — would best suit (his or her / their) needs. **6** After the gentle informational stage, one of the salespeople will begin (his or her / their) heavy sales pitch. **7** One widespread tactic used by salespeople is to make everybody think the product will never again be available to (him or her / them). **8** Some also use harassment techniques: (he or she / they) make anybody who does not agree to a purchase feel bad about (himself or herself / themselves). **9** Many salespeople will use the common practice of calling on the "big guns": (He or she brings / They bring) in a supervisor to make the customer feel guilty for wasting the sales representative's time. **10** Many of these "free gift" seminars are not really free: (It / They) often take more time than promised, and (it / they) can bring on stress and frustration.

Collective Nouns

A **collective noun** names a group that acts as a single unit. Some common collective nouns are *class, committee, company, family, government, group,* and *team.* Collective nouns are often singular, so when you use a pronoun to refer to a collective noun, it too must usually be singular.

INCORRECT

The class was assigned *their* first paper on Monday.

The team won *their* first victory in ten years.

CORRECT

The class was assigned *its* first paper on Monday.

[The class as a whole was assigned the paper, so the meaning is singular, and the singular pronoun *its* is used.]

The team won *its* first victory in ten years.

[The team, acting as one, had a victory, so the singular pronoun *its* is used.]

If the people in a group are acting separately, however, the noun is plural and should be used with a plural pronoun.

The audience shifted in *their* seats.

[The people shifted at different times in different seats. They were not acting as one.]

PRACTICE 2

In each of the following sentences, circle the correct pronoun in parentheses.

1 In March, the corporation made (their/its) decision to move to a new office in the town of Lawson. **2** The town council gave (their/its) wholehearted approval to the project. **3** The community invited the executives to (their/its) annual spring barbecue. **4** A construction company was chosen to build the factory, and (it/they) began the project in May. **5** Each department will now have (their/its) own kitchen facility. **6** The administrative group will have (their/its) choice of break rooms. **7** The board of directors moved into (their/its) offices yesterday, and the rest of the company will follow next week. **8** A large crowd will be invited to the grand opening, and (their/its) seats will be arranged around a green space in front of the building.

Make Pronoun References Clear

A pronoun should refer to only one noun, and it should be clear what that noun is.

> **CONFUSING**
>
> I put the shirt in the drawer, even though *it* was dirty.
> [Was the shirt or the drawer dirty?]
>
> If you cannot find your doctor's office, *they* can help.
> [Who are *they*?]
>
> An hour before the turkey was to be done, *it* broke.
> [What broke?]
>
> **CLEAR**
>
> I put the dirty shirt in the drawer.
>
> If you cannot find your doctor's office, *the information desk* can help.
>
> An hour before the turkey was to be done, *the oven* broke.

PRACTICE 3

Edit each sentence to eliminate problems with pronoun reference. Some sentences may be revised in more than one way.

> **EXAMPLE:** When we were young, our babysitter gave my sister Jan
> and me a book that became one of ~~her~~ *Jan's* favorites.

1. The babysitter, Jan, and I were fascinated by *Twenty Thousand Leagues under the Sea,* and she is now studying marine biology.

2. I know little about the ocean except for what it says in occasional magazine articles.

3. I enjoy visiting the aquarium and have taken a biology class, but it did not focus on ocean life as much as I would have liked.

4. I did learn that it covers about 71 percent of the earth's surface.

5. Both space and the ocean are largely unexplored, and it contains a huge proportion of all life on Earth.

6. They say that the ocean might contain as many as a million undiscovered species.

7. Jan says that they have found some odd creatures in the ocean.

8. In Indonesia, they have found an octopus that uses camouflage and "walks" across the ocean floor on two legs.

9. According to marine biologists who made the discovery, it looks like a piece of seaweed bouncing along the sand.

10. Scientists say that it might help them develop better robot arms.

A pronoun should replace the subject of a sentence, not repeat it.

PRONOUN REPEATS SUBJECT	TIP For more on subjects, verbs, and other sentence parts, see Chapter 8.

PRONOUN REPEATS SUBJECT

The doctor, *she* told me to take one aspirin a day.

The plane, *it* arrived on time despite the fog.

CORRECT

The doctor told me to take one aspirin a day.

The plane arrived on time despite the fog.

TIP For more on subjects, verbs, and other sentence parts, see Chapter 8.

PRACTICE 4

Correct repetitious pronoun references in the following sentences.

> **EXAMPLE:** Many objects that we use today ~~they~~ were invented by the Chinese.

1. Fireworks they were originally used by the Chinese to scare enemies in war.

2. The wheelbarrow, also invented in China, it was called the "wooden ox."

3. People who use paper fans to cool off they should thank the Chinese for this invention.

4. The oldest piece of paper in the world it was discovered in China.

5. Matches were also invented in China when a woman she wanted an easier way to start fires for cooking.

Use the Right Pronoun Case

There are three pronoun cases: subject, object, and possessive. Subject pronouns act as the subject of a verb, object pronouns act as the object of a verb or preposition, and possessive pronouns show ownership.

SUBJECT PRONOUN	*She* entered the race.
	Dan got nervous when *he* heard the news.
OBJECT PRONOUN	Shane gave *her* the keys.
	Marla went to the store with *them*.
POSSESSIVE PRONOUN	*My* feet hurt.
	The puppies are now *yours*.

TIP For more on pronoun case, see pages 83–84.

Choosing between subject and object case can be especially difficult in:

- sentences with more than one subject or object,
- sentences that make a comparison, and
- sentences that use *who* or *whom*.

SENTENCES WITH MORE THAN ONE SUBJECT OR OBJECT

When a subject or an object has more than one part, it is called **compound**. The parts are joined by *and* or *or*.

COMPOUND SUBJECT	Travis and *I* play soccer.
	[The two subjects are *Travis* and *I*.]
COMPOUND OBJECT	Becky made the candles for the boys and *me*.
	[The two objects are *boys* and *me*.]

To decide what type of pronoun is correct in your sentence, underline the subject(s), double-underline the verb, and circle any objects (words that receive the action of the verb).

If there is a compound subject, such as *Daniella and me*, or a compound object, such as *Jack and I*, cross out one of the subjects or objects so that only the pronoun remains.

PRONOUN ERROR	~~Daniella and~~ me go running every morning.
	The waiter brought the dessert tray to ⟨Jack⟩ and I.

If the sentence sounds wrong with just the pronoun as the subject or object it must be revised. *Me go running every morning* and *The waiter brought the dessert tray to I* both sound wrong and need to be fixed.

              I
Daniella and ~~me~~ go running every morning.

The waiter brought the dessert tray to Jack and ~~I~~. *me*

Personal Pronouns

	SUBJECT		OBJECT		POSSESSIVE	
	Singular	Plural	Singular	Plural	Singular	Plural
First Person	I	we	me	us	my / mine	our / ours
Second Person	you	you	you	you	your / yours	your / yours
Third Person	he / she / it	they	him / her / it	them	his / her / hers / its	their / theirs

TIP When you are writing about yourself and someone else, always put yourself after everyone else. *My friends and I went to the movies,* not *I and my friends went to the movies.*

INCORRECT

Harold and *me* like to go to the races.

The boss gave the hardest job to Rico and *I.*

I sent the e-mail to Ellen and *she.*

CORRECT

Harold and *I* like to go to the races.

[Think: *I* like to go to the races.]

The boss gave the hardest job to Rico and *me.*

[Think: The boss gave the hardest job to *me.*]

I sent the e-mail to Ellen and *her.*

[Think: I sent the e-mail to *her.*]

Many people make the mistake of writing *between you and I.* It should be *between you and me.*

The girl sat between you and ~~I~~ *me*.

. . . .

PRACTICE 5

Circle the correct pronoun in each of the following sentences.

EXAMPLE: When I was eight, my parents got a surprise for my sister

Lara and (I /(me)).

1. When Dad got home from work, Mom and (he/him) left for the mall, but my sister Lara and I did not get to go with them.

2. (Her/She) and I had begged for a pet for months.

3. Our parents were tired of our pleas and got (we/us) a hamster at the mall pet store.

4. I was happy even though (we/us) had hoped for a puppy.

5. My aunt arrived with an old aquarium that she gave to my sister and (I/me).

6. We set it up for our hamster and called Dominic, my best friend, to tell (he/him) about our new pet.

7. Several days later, something happened that surprised (we/us).

8. Lara ran into the room crying and told (I/me) that little pink things had gotten into the aquarium.

9. I ran to look at (they/them) and counted eight baby hamsters.

10. Between you and (I/me), I think my parents were sorry they did not get us a puppy.

PRONOUNS USED IN COMPARISONS

A **comparison** describes similarities and differences between two things. It often includes the words *than* or *as*.

Terrence is happier *than* Elena.

Terrence is as happy *as* Carla.

Pronouns have specific meanings in comparisons, so be sure to use the right ones. To do so, mentally add the words that are missing.

Subject (of *I like video games*)

Ann likes video games more than *I*.

[This sentence means "Ann likes video games more than I like them." You can tell by adding the missing words to the end: *more than I **like video games**.*]

Object (of *she likes me*)

Ann likes video games more than *me*.

[This sentence means "Ann likes video games more than she likes me." You can tell by adding the missing words to the end: *more than **she likes** me.*]

Check your writing for any sentences with comparisons and circle the word that signals a comparison (*than* or *as*).

PRONOUN   April studies more (than) me.
ERROR

Ask what word or words could be added to complete the comparison. In the above example, *study* could be added. Then ask whether the sentence makes sense with the added word(s). [*April studies more than me study* does not make sense.]

I (study)
April studies more than ~~me~~.
              ^

INCORRECT

Bettina is taller than *me*.

I wish I could sing as well as *her*.

Our neighbors are quieter than *us*.

CORRECT

Bettina is taller than *I*.
[Think: Bettina is taller than *I* am.]

I wish I could sing as well as *she*.
[Think: I wish I could sing as well as *she* sings.]

Our neighbors are quieter than *we*.
[Think: Our neighbors are quieter than *we* are.]

PRACTICE 6

Edit each sentence using the correct pronoun case. One sentence is correct; write **C** next to it.

> **EXAMPLE:** When MTV's Video Music Awards are on every year,
>
>   *I*
> nobody gets more excited than ~~me~~.
>   ^

1. There are many awards shows, but none are as fun and unpredictable as them.

2. My friends watch the show with me even though they don't like music as much as me.

3. My boyfriend enjoys watching it too, although I know much more than him about pop music.

4. My boyfriend sometimes jokes that he is jealous and says that I like MTV more than he.

5. The performances on the VMA show are always great; there is nothing I like better than they.

6. Because the VMA show is live, there are often unplanned stunts, and some people are more interested in they than the music.

7. For example, when Taylor Swift won Best Female Video award in 2009, nobody was more surprised than she at what happened.

8. Kanye West interrupted Swift during her acceptance speech because he thought another singer deserved the award more than her.

9. I have never seen a singer as embarrassed as her after that.

10. When the audience booed him, however, West realized that other people did not feel the same as him.

....

WHO VERSUS WHOM

Who is always a subject; use it if the pronoun performs an action. *Whom* is always an object; use it if the pronoun does not perform any action.

WHO = SUBJECT	Dennis is the neighbor *who* helped us build the deck.
	[*Who* (*Dennis*) is the subject.]
WHOM = OBJECT	Carol is the woman *whom* I met at school.
	[You can turn the sentence around: *I met whom* (*Carol*) *at school. Whom* (*Carol*) is the object of the verb *met*.]

In most cases, for sentences in which the pronoun is followed by a verb, use *who*. When the pronoun is followed by a noun or pronoun, use *whom*.

The man (**who**/ whom) called 911 was unusually calm.
[The pronoun is followed by the verb *called*. Use *who*.]

The woman (who /**whom**) I drove to the train was from Turkey.
[The pronoun is followed by another pronoun: *I*. Use *whom*.]

Whoever is a subject pronoun; *whomever* is an object pronoun.

....

PRACTICE 7

In each sentence, circle the correct word, *who* or *whom*.

EXAMPLE: Mary Frith was a thief (**who**/ whom) lived in the 1600s.

1. She joined a gang of thieves (who/whom) were known as cutpurses.

2. People (who/whom) had money and jewelry carried the items in purses tied around their waists.

3. Mary and her gang would cut the purse strings, steal the purses, and find someone to (who/whom) they could sell the goods.

4. Mary, (who/whom) was not one to pass up a chance to make money, opened her own shop to sell the "used" goods.

5. She often sold items back to the people from (who/whom) she had stolen them.

. . . .

PRACTICE 8

Read the following paragraph and correct the pronoun errors. Two sentences are correct; write **C** next to them.

1 Sometimes, a student receives a grade that is not what they expected for a course. **2** To help students determine whether the grade is correct, they usually have a policy for challenging grades. **3** Although the policies may differ among schools, most schools require that students follow a series of steps. **4** First, anyone who is concerned about a grade should contact their instructor to ask for an explanation. **5** The student should provide copies of quizzes, tests, research papers, or other assignments as evidence. **6** If him or her and the instructor cannot reach a compromise, it might be brought to a higher authority, such as a department committee. **7** The committee will issue their ruling after contacting the student and instructor for information. **8** Based on the ruling, the original grade it will either stand or be changed. **9** No one is happier than us administrators when both parties feel they have been treated fairly. **10** Just remember: Students whom want to challenge a grade usually have a limited time in which to do so.

. . . .

Adjectives and Adverbs

TIP For a review of these parts of speech, see page 89.

Adjectives describe nouns and pronouns. They add information about what kind, which one, or how many.

Maria is **tired**.

Maria works **two** shifts and takes **three** classes.

Maria babysits for her **younger** sister.

Adverbs describe verbs, adjectives, or other adverbs. They add information about how, how much, when, where, or why. Adverbs often end with -*ly*.

Stephan **accidentally** banged his toe on the table.

He was **extremely** late for work.

His toe became swollen **very** quickly.

Choose between Adjectives and Adverbs

Many adverbs are formed by adding *-ly* to the end of an adjective.

ADJECTIVE	ADVERB
The *fresh* vegetables glistened in the sun.	The house was *freshly* painted.
She is an *honest* person.	She answered the question *honestly*.

INCORRECT

I was *real* pleased about the news.

We saw an *extreme* funny show last night.

We had a *peacefully* view of the lake.

TIP Note that nouns can be used as adjectives — for example, *City traffic is terrible.*

CORRECT

I was *really* pleased about the news.
[An adverb, *really,* describes the verb *pleased.*]

We saw an *extremely* funny show last night.
[An adverb, *extremely,* describes the adjective *funny.*]

We had a *peaceful* view of the lake.
[An adjective, *peaceful,* describes the noun *view.*]

PRACTICE 9

Choose an adjective or adverb, as indicated, to fill in each blank in the sentences below.

1. I swam _____ across the pond. (Adverb)

2. The _____ sunset bathed the beach in a red glow. (Adjective)

3. The _____ old house scared the children. (Adjective)

4. If the train arrives _____, call me for a ride. (Adverb)

5. The _____ dog chased every car on the street. (Adjective)

Adjectives and Adverbs in Comparisons

To compare two persons, places, things, or ideas, use the **comparative** form of adjectives or adverbs. This form often includes *than*.

> Trina runs *faster* than I do.

> Davio dances *more gracefully* than Harper does.

To compare three or more persons, places, things, or ideas, use the **superlative** form of adjectives or adverbs.

> Trina runs the *fastest* of all our friends.

> Davio is the *most graceful* of all the ballroom dancers.

Comparative and Superlative Forms

ADVERBS AND ADJECTIVES OF ONE SYLLABLE: Add *-er* to form the comparative and *-est* to form the superlative.

ADJECTIVE OR ADVERB	COMPARATIVE	SUPERLATIVE
tall	taller	tallest
fast	faster	fastest

EXAMPLE   Miguel is the *tallest* boy in the class.

ADJECTIVES ENDING IN -y: Follow the same rule as for one-syllable words, but change the *-y* to *-i* before adding *-er* or *-est*.

ADJECTIVE OR ADVERB	COMPARATIVE	SUPERLATIVE
happy	happier	happiest
silly	sillier	silliest

EXAMPLE   That is the *silliest* joke I have ever heard.

ADVERBS AND ADJECTIVES OF MORE THAN ONE SYLLABLE: Add *more* to make the comparative and *most* to make the superlative.

ADJECTIVE OR ADVERB	COMPARATIVE	SUPERLATIVE
graceful	more graceful	most graceful
gracefully	more gracefully	most gracefully
intelligent	more intelligent	most intelligent
intelligently	more intelligently	most intelligently

EXAMPLE   Last night's debate was the *most intelligent* one I have ever seen.

TIP Think of a syllable as a "beat": the word *adjective* has three beats, or syllables.

TIP For more on changing a final *-y* to *-i* when adding endings, and on other spelling changes involving endings, see Chapter 14.

Use either an ending (*-er* or *-est*) or an extra word (*more* or *most*) to form a comparative or superlative—not both at once.

> Some say that Dale Earnhardt was the ~~most~~ greatest NASCAR driver ever.

....

PRACTICE 10

Write the comparative and superlative form of the adjective or adverb.

EXAMPLES:	tall	*taller, tallest*
	beautiful	*more beautiful, most beautiful*

1. smart   **5.** brief   **8.** funny

2. strong   **6.** wealthy   **9.** thankful

3. quietly   **7.** patiently   **10.** normal

4. joyful

....

Good, Well, Bad, and Badly

Good, well, bad, and *badly* do not follow the regular rules for forming comparatives and superlatives.

Forms of *Good, Well, Bad,* and *Badly*

ADJECTIVE	COMPARATIVE	SUPERLATIVE
good	better	best
bad	worse	worst
ADVERB	**COMPARATIVE**	**SUPERLATIVE**
well	better	best
badly	worse	worst

People often get confused about whether to use *good* or *well*. *Good* is an adjective, so use it to describe a noun or pronoun. *Well* is an adverb, so use it to describe a verb or an adjective.

ADJECTIVE	Mike is a *good* person.
	[The adjective *good* describes the noun *person*.]
ADVERB	He works *well* with others.
	[The adverb *well* describes the verb *works*.]

Well can also be an adjective to describe someone's health.

INCORRECT	Louisa is not feeling *good* today, so she might not run well.
CORRECT	Louisa is not feeling *well* today, so she might not run well.

PRACTICE 11

In each of the following sentences, underline the word that *good* or *well* modifies, and then circle the correct word in parentheses.

> **EXAMPLE:** For some people, the fields of hair care, cosmetology, and wellness are (good/ well) career choices.

1. The ability to communicate (good/well) can be the difference between being a successful and an unsuccessful beauty consultant.

2. Another important characteristic for beauty-care workers is to be (good/well) in creative areas such as art and graphic design.

3. People with artistic talent and a strong sense of visual style usually do (good/well) in the beauty industry.

4. One thing that beauty professionals love about their work is that they get to make their clients feel (good/well) about themselves.

5. Another benefit of working in the beauty industry, especially hair care, is that it is always necessary, whether the economy is performing (good/well) or badly.

PRACTICE 12

In each of the following sentences, underline the word that is being described. Then, circle the correct comparative or superlative form of *good* or *bad* in parentheses.

> EXAMPLE: When combined with regular exercise, a healthful
>
> breakfast is one of the (better /(best)) ways to stay fit.

1. What is the (better/best) beverage to drink in the morning?

2. Orange juice is (better/best) than coffee, but plain water is the healthiest choice.

3. What is the (worse/worst) type of breakfast food?

4. Doughnuts are much (worse/worst) than some kinds of cereal.

5. A fiber-rich food that contains B vitamins is among the (better/best) breakfast foods.

PRACTICE 13

Edit the adjectives and adverbs in the following paragraph. Two sentences are correct; write **C** next to them.

 1 College tuition costs are more higher than ever before. 2 At Merriweather College, financial aid advisers are available to help students understand the different types of financial aid available. 3 The commonest types of aid include scholarships, loans, and military aid. 4 Scholarships exist for students who perform good in academics or athletics. 5 Scholarships are also available for students specializing in fields such as agriculture or nursing. 6 For many students, government loans are gooder than private loans. 7 Government loans do not require credit checks, and they usual offer the lowest interest rates. 8 The popularest loans are the Stafford and the Perkins. 9 Finally, students can enroll in Reserve Officers Training Corps (ROTC) for funds, and veterans can also obtain well tuition benefits. 10 Students with questions should contact the financial aid department, and a meeting with an adviser will be set up quick.

Misplaced and Dangling Modifiers

Modifiers are words or word groups that describe other words in a sentence.

The man *who came in late* is Marlee's father.

[The words *who came in late* modify *man*.]

Unless the modifier is near the words it describes, the sentence can be confusing or funny.

Misplaced Modifiers

A **misplaced modifier** is placed incorrectly in the sentence and ends up describing the wrong word or words.

MISPLACED	Risa saw Sanjay's cat *standing on a ladder*.
	[Was Sanjay's cat standing on a ladder? No, Risa was standing on a ladder, so the modifier must come right before or right after her name.]
CORRECT	*Standing on a ladder,* Risa saw Sanjay's cat.

Four types of modifiers are often misplaced:

- **Modifiers such as *only, almost, hardly, nearly,* and *just***

  I ~~only~~ drove *only* thirty miles on my vacation.

- **Modifiers that start with *-ing* verbs**

  Opening the closet, Candice found her daughter's hamster. ~~opening the closet.~~

- **Modifiers that are prepositional phrases**

  I found the bill *from the dry cleaner* in the drawer. ~~from the dry cleaner.~~

- **Modifiers that are clauses starting with *who, whose, that,* or *which***

  Babysitters *who play with children* are the most popular. ~~who play with children.~~

Dangling Modifiers

A **dangling modifier** "dangles" because the word or words that it is supposed to describe are not in the sentence. A dangling modifier is usually at the beginning of the sentence and seems to modify the noun after it, but it really does not.

DANGLING	*Looking under the dresser,* a dust ball went up my nose.
	[Was the dust ball looking under the dresser? No.]
CORRECT	*Looking under the dresser,* I inhaled a dust ball.
	[The correction adds the word being modified right after the opening modifier.]
CORRECT	While I was *looking under the dresser,* a dust ball went up my nose.
	[The correction adds the word being modified to the opening modifier itself.]

PRACTICE 14

Edit the modifiers in the following passage. Two sentences are correct; write **C** next to them.

1 Free credit report scams nearly are everywhere. **2** An ad might give the impression that a certain Web site gives free credit report information on television. **3** Sent directly to your inbox, companies make convincing arguments that your credit score is doomed unless you act fast. **4** The most frustrating thing is that these credit report sites claim to be free.

5 In reality, the federal government has only authorized one site, AnnualCreditReport.com, to provide people with a free credit report each year. **6** The other sites all almost charge a fee to get the "free" report. **7** The unauthorized sites also lure in unsuspecting customers requiring a minimum subscription to their monthly reports.

8 Understanding that many ads are misleading, fraud claims are being investigated by the government. **9** Caused by past credit history, a person cannot adjust a low score just by visiting a Web site. **10** The best things you can do to improve your credit score are paying your bills on time and getting out of debt.

14

Style, Word Choice, and Spelling

Writing Effective Sentences

Avoid Choppy Sentences

If all your sentences are short, they will seem choppy and hard to read. There are two common ways to combine two short sentences into one longer one: coordination and subordination.

Coordination

In **coordination**, two sentences with closely related ideas are joined into a single sentence, either with a comma and a coordinating conjunction or with a semicolon.

TWO SENTENCES, UNRELATED IDEAS	It was hot today. My neighbor called to ask me to stay with her baby. [These sentences should not be combined because the ideas are not related.]
TWO SENTENCES, RELATED IDEAS	Today, my son got an iPad and a new computer. He is using them right now.
COMBINED THROUGH COORDINATION	Today, my son got an iPad and a new computer, *and* he is using them right now. [The sentences are joined with a comma and the coordinating conjunction *and*.]
COMBINED THROUGH COORDINATION	Today, my son got an iPad and a new computer; he is using them right now. [The sentences are joined with a semicolon.]

LearningCurve **For extra practice in the skills covered in this chapter, visit bedfordstmartins.com/rsinteractive.**

COORDINATING CONJUNCTIONS

One way to join independent clauses (complete sentences) is by using a comma and a **coordinating conjunction**. You can remember the coordinating conjunctions by thinking of *fanboys:* **f**or, **a**nd, **n**or, **b**ut, **o**r, **y**et, **s**o. Do not choose just any conjunction; choose the one that makes the most sense.

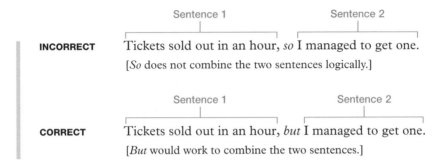

	Sentence 1		Sentence 2
INCORRECT	Tickets sold out in an hour, *so* I managed to get one.		
	[*So* does not combine the two sentences logically.]		

	Sentence 1		Sentence 2
CORRECT	Tickets sold out in an hour, *but* I managed to get one.		
	[*But* would work to combine the two sentences.]		

Here are the meanings of the coordinating conjunctions and more examples of their use:

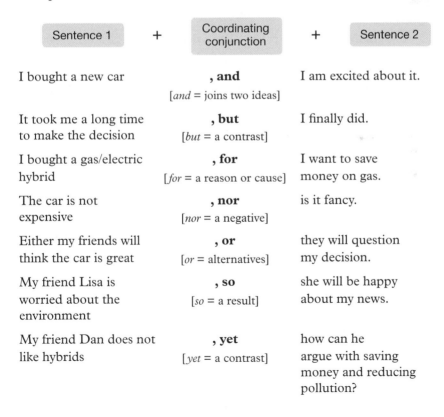

Sentence 1	+	Coordinating conjunction	+	Sentence 2
I bought a new car		**, and** [*and* = joins two ideas]		I am excited about it.
It took me a long time to make the decision		**, but** [*but* = a contrast]		I finally did.
I bought a gas/electric hybrid		**, for** [*for* = a reason or cause]		I want to save money on gas.
The car is not expensive		**, nor** [*nor* = a negative]		is it fancy.
Either my friends will think the car is great		**, or** [*or* = alternatives]		they will question my decision.
My friend Lisa is worried about the environment		**, so** [*so* = a result]		she will be happy about my news.
My friend Dan does not like hybrids		**, yet** [*yet* = a contrast]		how can he argue with saving money and reducing pollution?

TIP To do this chapter, you need to know how compound and complex sentences work. For a review, see Chapter 8.

PRACTICE 1

In each of the following sentences, fill in the blank with an appropriate coordinating conjunction. There may be more than one correct answer for some sentences.

> **EXAMPLE:** Most workers receive only two to three weeks of vacation
>
> a year, _____ *so* _____ they choose their vacation
>
> destinations carefully.

1. Las Vegas is one of the hottest vacation spots in America,

   _____ it is not just because of the warm, sunny

   weather.

2. Las Vegas is famous for its casinos, _____ there is

   more to the city than many people think.

3. You can browse in the many shops, _____ you can

   relax in a cool swimming pool.

4. The MGM Grand Hotel has a lion's den, _____ the

   Bellagio presents a beautiful fountain show every fifteen minutes in

   the evenings.

5. Many tourists who visit Las Vegas do not like gambling,

   _____ they can have a wonderful time there.

SEMICOLONS

Another method of combining related sentences is to use a **semicolon (;)** between them. Occasional semicolons are fine, but do not overuse them.

Sentence 1	;	Sentence 2
My favorite hobby is bike riding	;	it is the best way to see the country.

It is faster than running but slower than driving	;	that is the perfect speed for me.

A semicolon alone does not tell readers much about how the two ideas are related. Use a **conjunctive adverb** after the semicolon to give more information about the relationship. Put a comma after the conjunctive adverb.

Equal idea	+	Conjunctive adverb	+	Equal idea

; afterward,
; also,
; as a result,

Equal idea	+	Conjunctive adverb	+	Equal idea

; besides,
; consequently,
; frequently,
; however,
; in addition,
; in fact,
; instead,
; still,
; then,
; therefore,

I ride my bike a lot	; as a result,	I am in good enough shape for a long-distance ride.
My boyfriend wants me to go on a bike tour with him	; however,	I would find that stressful.
I ride my bike to relax	; therefore,	I suggested that he take a friend on the tour.

PRACTICE 2

Join each pair of sentences by using a semicolon alone.

> **EXAMPLE:** Some foods are not meant to be eaten by themselves.
> *macaroni*
> ~~Macaroni~~ would be no fun without cheese.

1.   Homemade chocolate chip cookies are delicious. They even better with a glass of cold milk.

2.   A hamburger by itself seems incomplete. It needs a pile of fries to be truly satisfying.

3.   Fries have another natural partner. Most people like to eat them with ketchup.

4.   Apple pie is just apple pie. Add a scoop of vanilla ice cream, and you have an American tradition.

5.   A peanut butter sandwich is boring. A little jelly adds some excitement.

Subordination

Like coordination, **subordination** is a way to combine short, choppy sentences with related ideas into a longer sentence. With subordination, you put a dependent word (such as *after, although, because,* or *when*) in front of one of the sentences. The resulting sentence will have one complete sentence and one dependent clause, which is no longer a complete sentence.

Before you join two sentences, make sure they have closely related ideas.

TWO SENTENCES, UNRELATED IDEAS	I was hospitalized after a car accident. I had a pizza for lunch.
	[These two sentences should not be combined because the ideas are not related.]
TWO SENTENCES, RELATED IDEAS	I was hospitalized after a car accident. My friends showed me how supportive they could be.
JOINED THROUGH SUBORDINATION	*When* I was hospitalized after a car accident, my friends showed me how supportive they could be.
	[The dependent word *when* logically combines the two sentences. The underlined word group is a dependent clause, and the second word group is a complete sentence.]

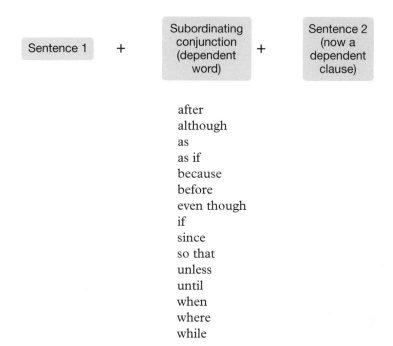

after
although
as
as if
because
before
even though
if
since
so that
unless
until
when
where
while

TIP The word *subordinate* means "lower in rank" or "secondary." In the workplace, for example, you are subordinate to your boss. In the army, a private is subordinate to an officer.

Choose the conjunction that makes the most sense with the two sentences.

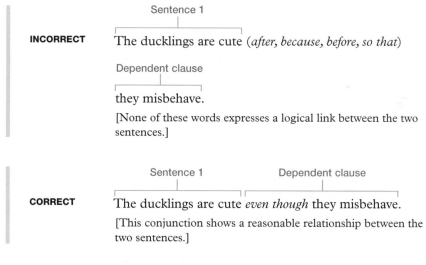

Sentence 1

INCORRECT   The ducklings are cute (*after, because, before, so that*)

Dependent clause

they misbehave.

[None of these words expresses a logical link between the two sentences.]

Sentence 1   Dependent clause

CORRECT   The ducklings are cute *even though* they misbehave.

[This conjunction shows a reasonable relationship between the two sentences.]

When the *complete sentence* is before the dependent clause, do not use a comma. However, when the *dependent clause* is before the complete sentence, put a comma after it.

TIP When you join sentences with subordination, watch out for misplaced and dangling modifiers. See Chapter 13.

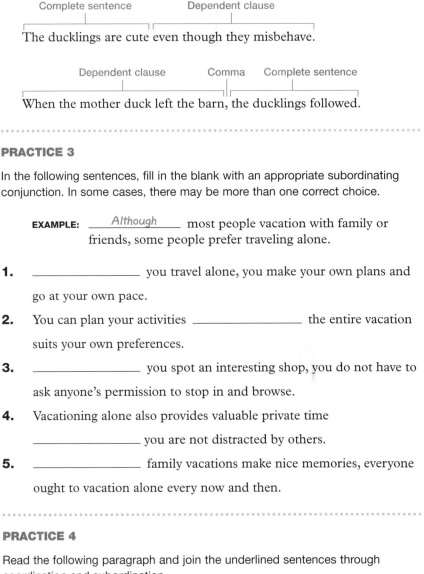

Complete sentence   Dependent clause

The ducklings are cute even though they misbehave.

Dependent clause   Comma   Complete sentence

When the mother duck left the barn, the ducklings followed.

PRACTICE 3

In the following sentences, fill in the blank with an appropriate subordinating conjunction. In some cases, there may be more than one correct choice.

EXAMPLE: _____*Although*_____ most people vacation with family or friends, some people prefer traveling alone.

1. _____ you travel alone, you make your own plans and go at your own pace.

2. You can plan your activities _____ the entire vacation suits your own preferences.

3. _____ you spot an interesting shop, you do not have to ask anyone's permission to stop in and browse.

4. Vacationing alone also provides valuable private time _____ you are not distracted by others.

5. _____ family vacations make nice memories, everyone ought to vacation alone every now and then.

PRACTICE 4

Read the following paragraph and join the underlined sentences through coordination and subordination.

 1 Type 2 diabetes is also known as adult-onset or non-insulin-dependent diabetes. **2** Most diabetes cases are classified as Type 2 diabetes. **3** Ninety to 95 percent of diabetics have this type of the disease. **4** Without treatment, Type 2 diabetes can lead to a wide range of complications. **5** In fact, diabetes is the fifth-deadliest disease in the United States. **6** It can be controlled or even prevented by careful attention to diet and exercise. **7** Patients should be encouraged to exercise for thirty minutes daily. **8** They should be taught how to plan meals according to the American Diabetes Association's Diabetes Food Pyramid. **9** It is also important for patients to practice proper foot and skin care. **10** Diabetes can cause skin infections, particularly on the feet. **11** Without proper care, skin infections can lead to serious complications and even amputation. **12** Smoking is especially dangerous for people with diabetes. **13** Smokers should be provided with resources to help them quit. **14** Living with diabetes is not easy. **15** Patients can live long and healthy lives if they receive education and support in controlling the disease.

Balance Parallel Ideas

Parallelism in writing means that similar parts of a sentence have the same structure: nouns are with nouns, verbs with verbs, and phrases with phrases.

Read the following sentences, emphasizing the underlined parts. Can you hear the problems with parallelism? Can you hear how the corrections help?

NOT PARALLEL	Caitlin likes history more than studying math.
	[*History* is a noun, but *studying math* is a phrase.]
PARALLEL	Caitlin likes history more than math.
NOT PARALLEL	The performers sang, danced, and were doing magic tricks.
	[*Were doing* is not in the same form as the other verbs.]
PARALLEL	The performers sang, danced, and did magic tricks.
NOT PARALLEL	I would rather go to my daughter's soccer game than sitting in the town meeting.
	[*To my daughter's soccer game* and *sitting in the town meeting* are both phrases, but they have different forms.]
PARALLEL	I would rather go to my daughter's soccer game than to the town meeting.

Parallelism in Pairs and Lists

When two or more items in a series are joined by *and* or *or*, use the same form for each item.

> **NOT PARALLEL**   The state fair featured a <u>rodeo</u> and <u>having a pie-eating contest</u>.
>
> [*Rodeo*, the first of the pair of items, is a noun, so the second item should also be a noun. *Having a pie-eating contest* is more than just a noun, so the pair is not parallel.]

> **PARALLEL**   The state fair featured a <u>rodeo</u> and a <u>pie-eating contest</u>.
>
> [*Rodeo* and *pie-eating contest* are both nouns, so they are parallel.]

> **NOT PARALLEL**   The neighborhood group picked up trash <u>from deserted property</u>, <u>from parking lots</u>, and <u>they cleaned up the riverbank</u>.
>
> [The first two underlined items in the list have the same structure (*from . . .*), but the third is different (*they cleaned . . .*).]

> **PARALLEL**   The neighborhood group picked up trash <u>from deserted property</u>, <u>from parking lots</u>, and <u>from the riverbank</u>.
>
> [All items in the list now have the same *from . . .* structure.]

Parallelism in Comparisons

Comparisons often use the words *than* or *as*. To be parallel, the items on either side of the comparison word(s) need to have the same structure. In the examples that follow, the comparison word(s) are circled.

> **NOT PARALLEL**   Learning how to play the drums is (as hard as) the guitar.

> **PARALLEL**   Learning how to play the drums is (as hard as) learning how to play the guitar.

> **NOT PARALLEL**   Swimming is easier on your joints (than) a run.

> **PARALLEL**   Swimming is easier on your joints (than) running.

> **OR**   A swim is easier on your joints (than) a run.

To make the parts of a sentence parallel, you may need to add or drop a word or two.

NOT PARALLEL	A weekend trip can sometimes be (as restful as) going on a long vacation.
PARALLEL, WORD ADDED	**Taking** a weekend trip can sometimes be (as restful as) going on a long vacation.

NOT PARALLEL	Each month, my bill for day care is (more than) to pay my rent bill.
PARALLEL, WORDS DROPPED	Each month, my bill for day care is (more than) my bill.

Parallelism with Certain Paired Words

When a sentence uses certain paired words, the items joined by these words must be parallel. Here are common ones:

both . . . and	neither . . . nor	rather . . . than
either . . . or	not only . . . but also	

NOT PARALLEL	Tasha *both* cuts hair *and* she gives pedicures.
PARALLEL	Tasha *both* cuts hair *and* gives pedicures.

NOT PARALLEL	We would *rather* stay home *than* going dancing.
PARALLEL	We would *rather* stay home *than* go dancing.

· ·

PRACTICE 5

Fix problems with parallelism in the following paragraph. Two sentences are correct; write **C** next to them.

1 Since the 1970s, law enforcement's approach to domestic-violence calls has changed. **2** In the past, police often would neither make arrests nor would they record detailed information on the incident. **3** Resolving a domestic-abuse call commonly involved "cooling off" the abuser by walking him around the block or to talk to him privately.

4 In the late 1970s, however, approaches to partner abuse changed because of research findings and pressure from victims' advocates was increased. **5** Police agencies began to develop policies and programs for dealing with domestic incidents. **6** Today, police who respond to domestic-violence reports usually follow not only formal department guidelines but also there are statewide policies. **7** In some states, the criminal-justice system attempts to protect abuse survivors by pursuing cases even if the alleged victim does not show up in court or is not wanting to press charges. **8** Despite increased training and developing clearer policies, police officers often face unclear situations. **9** For example, when they arrive on the scene, officers may find that the allegedly abusive spouse is absent or discovering that the partner who made the call says that nothing happened. **10** Most officers today would rather record every detail of a domestic incident than risking being charged with failing to enforce domestic-violence laws.

Avoid Common Word-Choice Problems

Five common problems with word choice—vague words, slang, wordy language, clichés, and sexist language—can make it difficult for readers to understand you.

Vague Words

Your words need to create a clear picture for your readers. **Vague words** are too general to make an impression. The following are some common vague words.

Vague Words			
a lot	dumb	old	very
amazing	good	pretty	whatever
awesome	great	sad	young
bad	happy	small	
beautiful	nice	terrible	
big	OK (okay)	thing	

When you see one of these words or another general word in your writing, try to replace it with a concrete, or more specific, word. A concrete word names something that can be seen, heard, felt, tasted, or smelled.

VAGUE	The cookies were good.
CONCRETE	The cookies were warm, chewy, and sweet and had a rich, buttery taste.

The first version is too general. The second version creates a clear, strong impression.

Slang

Slang, informal language, and the abbreviations of text messaging should be used only in casual situations. Avoid them when you write for college classes or at work.

SLANG

I *wanna hang out* with you this weekend.

Dude, time to leave.

Sasha showed off her *bling* at the party.

This cell phone is *busted.*

EDITED

I *would like to spend time* with you this weekend.

Joe [or whoever], it is time to leave.

Sasha showed off her *jewelry* at the party.

This cell phone is *broken.*

Wordy Language

Wordy language contains unnecessary words. Sometimes, people think that using big words or writing long sentences will make them sound smart and important. However, using too many words in a piece of writing can make the point weaker or harder to find.

WORDY	*A great number of* students complained about the long registration lines.
EDITED	*Many* students complained about the long registration lines.

| WORDY | *Due to the fact that* we arrived late to the meeting, we missed the first speaker. |

| EDITED | *Because* we arrived late to the meeting, we missed the first speaker. |

| WORDY | We cannot buy a car *at this point in time*. |

| EDITED | We cannot buy a car *now*. |

Sometimes, sentences are wordy because some words in them repeat others, as in the italicized parts of the first sentence below.

| REPETITIVE | Our dog is *hyper* and *overactive*. |

| EDITED | Our dog is hyper. |

Common Wordy Expressions

WORDY	EDITED
As a result of	Because
Due to the fact that	Because
In spite of the fact that	Although
It is my opinion that	I think (or just make the point)
In the event that	If
The fact of the matter is that	(Just state the point.)
A great number of	Many
At that time	Then
In this day and age	Now, Nowadays
At this point in time	Now
In this paper I will show that . . .	(Just make the point; do not announce it.)

Clichés

Clichés are phrases that have been used so often that people no longer pay attention to them. To make your point clearly and to get your readers' attention, replace clichés with fresh, specific language.

CLICHÉS

June *works like a dog*.

This dinner roll is *as hard as a rock*.

EDITED

June works at least sixty hours every week.

This dinner roll would make a good baseball.

Common Clichés

as big as a house	no way on earth
better late than never	110 percent
break the ice	playing with fire
the corporate ladder	raining cats and dogs
crystal clear	spoiled rotten
a drop in the bucket	starting from scratch
easier said than done	sweating blood (or bullets)
as hard as a rock	24/7
hell on earth	work like a dog
last but not least	worked his or her way up the ladder
as light as a feather	

Sexist Language

Language that favors one gender over another or that assumes that only one gender performs a certain role is called *sexist*. Avoid such language.

SEXIST

A doctor should politely answer *his* patients' questions.

[Not all doctors are male.]

REVISED

A doctor should politely answer *his or her* patients' questions.

Doctors should politely answer *their* patients' questions.

[The first revision changes *his* to *his or her* to avoid sexism. The second revision changes the subject to a plural noun (*Doctors*) so that a genderless pronoun (*their*) can be used.]

TIP See Chapter 13 for more advice on using pronouns.

· ·

PRACTICE 6

Edit the following paragraph for word choice. Two sentences are correct; write **C** next to them.

1 In the past few years, carbohydrates have gotten a lot of flak from the media. **2** Popular diets made us believe that carbohydrates were really bad. **3** Some people decided that there was no way on earth they would ever eat pasta again. **4** Lately, however, a great number of dieters have changed their minds. **5** Carbohydrates are starting to be recognized as an important part of a healthy diet because they are the main source of energy for humans. **6** Current research demonstrates that while too many carbohydrates can be bad news, eliminating them completely is not wise. **7** The fact of the matter is that people should include healthy carbohydrates such as fruits, vegetables, and whole grains in their daily diets. **8** The overall key to good nutrition is eating balanced meals. **9** It is my opinion that people can eat many types of foods as long as they do so in moderation. **10** Maintaining a proper diet is easier said than done, but being fit as a fiddle is worth the work.

· ·

Use Commonly Confused Words Correctly

Study the different meanings and spellings of the following twenty-seven sets of commonly confused words.

TIP The vowels in the alphabet are *a, e, i, o, u,* and sometimes *y.* All other letters are consonants.

A / AN / AND

a: a word used before a word that begins with a consonant sound (article)

A large brown bear pawed the tent.

an: a word used before a word that begins with a vowel sound (article)

An egg on toast is delicious for breakfast.

and: a word used to join two words (conjunction)

Patrice *and* Dylan dated for three months.

In my favorite children's poem, *an* owl *and a* pussy-cat floated in *a* boat.

ACCEPT / EXCEPT

accept: to agree to receive or admit (verb)

Please *accept* my sincere apology.

except: but, other than (preposition)

I like all the songs on this CD *except* the last one.

The store will *accept* all credit cards *except* the one that I am carrying.

ADVICE / ADVISE

advice: opinion (noun)

Can you give me some *advice* about which course to take?

advise: to give an opinion (verb)

A park ranger *advised* us not to approach wild animals.

Grandma *advised* us girls to wear dresses to the concert; her *advice* is sweet but old-fashioned.

TIP To understand this chapter, you will need to know what nouns, verbs, adjectives, adverbs, and prepositions are. For a review, see Chapter 7.

AFFECT / EFFECT

affect: to make an impact on, to change something (verb)

The rising gas prices will *affect* our vacation plans.

effect: a result (noun)

The drought will have an *effect* on the citrus crop.

The new retirement policy will *affect* all future employees, but it will have no *effect* on current employees.

ARE / OUR

are: exist (a form of the verb *be*)

Those yellow roses *are* beautiful.

our: a word used to show ownership (possessive pronoun)

Have you seen *our* new car?

Are you interested in seeing *our* vacation pictures?

BY / BUY

by: next to, before (preposition)

My trusty dog walks *by* my side.

I must finish my essay *by* Tuesday.

buy: to purchase (verb)

I need to *buy* a new washing machine.

By the time I was eighteen, I was living on my own and saving to *buy* a new car.

CONSCIENCE / CONSCIOUS

TIP Remember that one of the words is *con-science;* the other is not.

conscience: a personal sense of right and wrong (noun)

Tiffany's *conscience* made her turn in the wallet she found.

conscious: awake, aware (adjective)

I became *conscious* of a steadily increasing rattle in my car.

We cannot sell this product in good *conscience* since we are quite *conscious* that it is addictive.

FINE / FIND

fine: of high quality (adjective); feeling well (adverb); a penalty for breaking a law (noun)

Charles and Marilyn received a set of *fine* china as a wedding gift.

Mandy had only three hours of sleep, but she feels *fine*.

If you park in the faculty parking lot, expect a $10 *fine*.

find: to locate, to discover (verb)

I need to *find* my car keys.

Did you *find* the book interesting?

I *find* that my grandmother's *fine* wood furniture looks great in my house.

ITS / IT'S

its: a word used to show ownership (possesive pronoun)

The jury has reached *its* verdict.

it's: a contraction of the words *it* (pronoun) and *is* (verb)

Did you know that *it's* snowing outside?

It's clear that the dog has injured *its* paw.

TIP If you
are not sure
whether
to use *its*
or *it's* in a
sentence, try
substituting
it is. If the
sentence
does not
make sense
with *it is*, use
its.

KNEW / NEW / KNOW / NO

knew: understood, recognized (past tense of the verb *know*)

I *knew* you would get the job.

new: unused, recent, or just introduced (adjective)

I think Jill has a *new* boyfriend.

know: to understand, to have knowledge of (verb)

Do you *know* how to operate this DVD player?

no: a word used to form a negative (adverb or adjective)

We have *no* more eggs.

I *know* that *no* job is too hard for this *new* employee.

LOOSE / LOSE

loose: baggy, relaxed, not fixed in place (adjective)

The handle on this frying pan is *loose*.

lose: to misplace, to give up possession of (verb); to be defeated (verb)

I *lose* my mittens every winter.

Are we going to *lose* the game?

You will *lose* your trousers if your belt is too *loose*.

MIND / MINE

mind: to object to (verb); the thinking or feeling part of the brain (noun)

Do you *mind* if I change the TV channel?

I wanted to be a rock star, but I have changed my *mind*.

mine: belonging to me (possessive pronoun); a source of ore and minerals (noun)

I am afraid that the ringing cell phone is *mine.*

We visited an abandoned silver *mine* in Colorado.

The boss does not *mind* if I hire a friend of *mine* to clean our offices.

Enrique has made up his *mind* to move to Alaska and take over his grandfather's gold *mine.*

OF / HAVE

of: coming from, caused by, part of a group, made from (preposition)

One *of* the puppies is already weaned.

have: to possess (verb; also used as a helping verb)

We *have* two dogwood trees in our backyard.

TIP Do not use *of* after *could, would, should,* or *might.* Use *have* after those words.

You could *have* bought that computer for a lower price across town.

Three *of* our best basketball players *have* quit the team.

PASSED / PAST

passed: went by, went ahead (past tense of the verb *pass*)

We *passed* several slow-moving cars on the country road.

past: time that has gone by (noun); earlier (adjective); gone by, over, just beyond (preposition)

My grandparents often talked about the *past.*

Jim has been an engineer for the *past* six years.

We accidentally drove right *past* our exit.

As we drove *past* the historic settlement, we felt that we had *passed* into a different era—the *past.*

PEACE / PIECE

peace: a lack of disagreement, calm (noun)

The *peace* was disrupted when the cat attacked the dog.

piece: a part of something larger (noun)

All I had for breakfast was a *piece* of toast.

After that *piece* of chocolate fudge cake, I felt completely at *peace*.

PRINCIPAL / PRINCIPLE

principal: main (adjective); the head of a school or leader in an organization (noun)

The *principal* cause of the fire is still unknown.

Nobody likes to be summoned to the *principal's* office.

The request must be approved by a *principal* in the regional office.

principle: a standard of beliefs or behaviors (noun)

Her decision was based on strong moral *principles*.

We are seeking someone with high *principles* to be the next *principal*.

QUIET / QUITE / QUIT

quiet: soft in sound, not noisy (adjective)

The children, for once, were *quiet*.

quite: completely, very (adverb)

It is *quite* foggy outside.

quit: to stop (verb)

Kenneth finally *quit* the band.

After the birds *quit* singing, the forest grew *quiet* and *quite* eerie.

RIGHT / WRITE

right: correct (adjective); in a direction opposite from left (noun)

The *right* job is not easy to find.

His office is two doors down the hall on the *right*.

write: to put words on paper (verb)

You must *write* your name and address clearly.

Now is the *right* time to *write* your résumé.

SET / SIT

set: a collection of something (noun); to place an object somewhere (verb)

What am I going to do with my old *set* of encyclopedias?

Please *set* those groceries on the counter.

sit: to be supported by a chair or other surface (verb)

I wish those children would *sit* down and be quiet.

Set down that broom. Will you *sit* down and choose a *set* of dishes for Felicia's wedding gift?

SUPPOSE / SUPPOSED

suppose: to imagine or assume to be true (verb)

I *suppose* you are right.

Do you *suppose* that Jared has a girlfriend?

supposed: intended (past tense and past participle of the verb *suppose*)

We *supposed* that you had simply forgotten Chad's birthday.

I am *supposed* to leave by 6:00 p.m.

Suppose you lost your job. Who is *supposed* to pay your bills?

THAN / THEN

than: a word used to compare two or more things or persons (preposition)

Cooper is a stronger bicyclist *than* Mitchell is.

He likes apples more *than* peaches.

then: at a certain time, next in time (adverb)

First, I was late to class; *then,* my cell phone rang during the lecture.

Back *then,* I was happier *than* I am now.

THEIR / THERE / THEY'RE

their: a word used to show ownership (possessive pronoun)

My grandparents have sold *their* boat.

there: a word indicating existence (pronoun) or location (adverb)

There are four new kittens over *there*.

they're: a contraction of the words *they* (pronoun) and *are* (verb)

They're good friends of mine.

There is proof that *they're* stealing from *their* neighbors.

TIP If you are not sure whether to use *their* or *they're*, substitute *they are*. If the sentence does not make sense, use *their*.

THOUGH / THROUGH / THREW

though: however, nevertheless, in spite of (conjunction)

I bought the computer *though* it seemed overpriced.

through: finished with (adjective); from one side to the other (preposition)

After you are *through* with the computer, may I use it?

The tornado passed *through* the north side of town.

threw: hurled, tossed (past tense of the verb *throw*)

Elena *threw* her worn-out socks into the trash can.

Though Zak *threw* a no-hitter in his last baseball game, he said he was *through* with baseball.

TO / TOO / TWO

to: a word indicating a direction or movement (preposition); part of the infinitive form of a verb

We are driving *to* Denver tomorrow.

I tried *to* ride my bicycle up that hill.

too: also, more than enough, very (adverb)

I like chocolate *too*.

Our steaks were cooked *too* much.

That storm came *too* close to us.

two: the number between one and three (adjective)

Marcia gets *two* weeks of vacation a year.

We are simply *too* tired *to* drive for *two* more hours.

USE / USED

use: to employ or put into service (verb)

Are you going to *use* that computer?

used: past tense of the verb *use*. *Used to* can indicate a past fact or state, or it can mean "familiar with."

Mother *used* a butter knife as a screwdriver.

Marcus *used to* play baseball for a minor league team.

I am not *used to* traveling in small airplanes.

You can *use* my truck if you are *used to* driving a standard transmission.

WHO'S / WHOSE

who's: a contraction of the words *who is* or *who has* (pronoun and verb)

May I tell her *who's* calling?

Who's been eating my cereal?

whose: a word showing ownership (possessive pronoun)

I do not know *whose* music I like best.

Whose car is parked in my flower bed? *Who's* responsible for this crime?

YOUR / YOU'RE

your: a word showing ownership (possessive pronoun)

Is this *your* dog?

you're: a contraction of the words *you* (pronoun) and *are* (verb)

I hope *you're* coming to Deb's party tonight.

You're bringing *your* girlfriend to the company picnic, aren't you?

TIP If you are not sure whether to use *your* or *you're*, substitute *you are*. If the sentence does not make sense, use *your*.

PRACTICE 7

Edit misused words in the following paragraph. Each sentence has one error.

1 Is a career in criminal justice write for you? **2** The first thing to understand is that there are three principle levels of law enforcement: local, state, and federal. **3** Local officers enforce state and local laws within there city or county. **4** State law enforcement agents include state police, who's duties are chiefly investigative, and state troopers, who enforce state laws on highways. **5** In most cases, a person needs an associate's degree too work as either a local or state police officer. **6** Federal law enforcement agents include Secret Service agents an FBI agents. **7** Federal jobs can take longer to get then state and local jobs, and they usually require a bachelor's degree. **8** Most law enforcement jobs have great pay, good benefits, and excellent job security, but these careers our not for everyone. **9** All officers must perform difficult tasks, and they constantly see people at they're worst. **10** However, if your self-motivated and want to make a difference in people's lives, a career in law enforcement may be for you.

Follow These Steps to Better Spelling

Remember Ten Troublemakers

Writing teachers have identified the ten words in the following list as the words that students most commonly misspell.

INCORRECT	CORRECT
alot	**a** lo**t**
arg**ue**ment	arg**um**ent
defin**ate**, def**e**nite	definite
develop**e**	develop
lite	li**ght**
nec**e**sary, ne**se**sary	ne**cess**ary
rec**ie**ve	rec**ei**ve
sep**e**rate	sep**a**rate
sur**priz**e, sup**ri**se	surprise
unti**ll**	unti**l**

Defeat Your Personal Spelling Demons

Try some of the following techniques to defeat your spelling demons:

- Create an explanation or saying that will help you remember the correct spelling. For example, "*surprise* is no *prize*" may remind you to spell *surprise* with an *s*, not a *z*.

- Say each separate part (syllable) of the word out loud so that you do not miss any letters (*dis-ap-point-ment, Feb-ru-ar-y, prob-a-bly*). You can also say each letter of the word out loud.

- Write the word correctly ten times.
- Write a paragraph in which you use the word at least three times.
- Ask a partner to give you a spelling test.

Learn Seven Spelling Rules

The following seven rules can help you avoid or correct many spelling errors. Quickly review vowels and consonants before you read the rules:

VOWELS: a e i o u

CONSONANTS: b c d f g h j k l m n p q r s t v w x y z

The letter *y* can be either a vowel (when it sounds like the *y* in *fly* or *hungry*) or a consonant (when it sounds like the *y* in *yellow*).

RULE 1

I before *e*
Except after *c*.
Or when sounded like *a*
As in *neighbor* or *weigh*.

piece (*i* before *e*)

receive (except after *c*)

eight (sounds like *a*)

EXCEPTIONS: either, neither, foreign, height, seize, society, their, weird

RULE 2

When a word ends in *e*, drop the final *e* when adding an ending that begins with a vowel.

hop**e** + ing = hoping

imagin**e** + ation = imagination

When a word ends in *e*, keep the final *e* when adding an ending that begins with a consonant.

achiev**e** + ment = achievement

definit**e** + ly = definitely

EXCEPTIONS: argument, awful, truly (and others)

RULE 3

When adding an ending to a word that ends in *y*, change the *y* to *i* when a consonant comes before the *y*.

lonely + est = loneliest

ha**pp**y + er = happ**i**er

apolo**gy** + ize = apolo**gi**ze

like**ly** + hood = likelihood

Do not change the *y* when a vowel comes before the *y*.

boy + ish = bo**y**ish

pay + ment = pa**y**ment

survey + or = surve**y**or

buy + er = bu**y**er

EXCEPTIONS

1. When adding *-ing* to a word ending in *y*, always keep the *y*, even if a consonant comes before it: stu**dy** + ing = stu**dy**ing.

2. Other exceptions include *daily, said,* and *paid.*

RULE 4

When adding an ending that starts with a vowel to a one-syllable word, double the final consonant only if the word ends with a consonant-vowel-consonant.

trap + ed = trap**p**ed

drip + ing = drip**p**ing

fat + er = fat**t**er

fit + er = fit**t**er

Do not double the final consonant if the word ends with some other combination.

VOWEL-VOWEL-CONSONANT	VOWEL-CONSONANT-CONSONANT
clean + est = cleanest	**slick** + er = slicker
poor + er = poorer	**teach** + er = teacher
clear + ed = cleared	**last** + ed = lasted

RULE 5

When adding an ending that starts with a vowel to a word of two or more syllables, double the final consonant only if the word ends with a consonant-vowel-consonant and the stress is on the last syllable.

> ad**mit** + ing = admitting
>
> con**trol** + er = controller
>
> oc**cur** + ence = occurrence
>
> pre**fer** + ed = preferred
>
> com**mit** + ed = committed

Do not double the final consonant in other cases.

> problem + atic = problematic
>
> understand + ing = understanding
>
> offer + ed = offered

RULE 6

To change a verb form to the third-person singular (*he, she, it*), add *-s* to the base form of most regular verbs.

> walk + s = walks (*She **walks**.*)
>
> jump + s = jumps (*He **jumps**.*)
>
> arrive + s = arrives (*The train **arrives**.*)

Add *-es* to most verbs that end in *s, sh, ch,* or *x.*

> **push** + es = pushes (*She **pushes**.*)
>
> **fix** + es = fixes (*He **fixes**.*)
>
> miss + es = misses (*The man **misses** the train.*)

RULE 7

To form the plural of most regular nouns, including nouns that end in *o* preceded by a vowel, add *-s.*

> book + s = books
>
> college + s = colleges
>
> radio + s = radios
>
> stereo + s = stereos

Add -*es* to nouns that end in *s*, *sh*, *ch*, or *x*, and nouns that end in *o* preceded by a consonant.

class + es = class**es**

ben**ch** + es = benc**hes**

pota**to** + es = potato**es**

he**ro** + es = hero**es**

Certain nouns form the plural irregularly, meaning that there are no rules to follow. The easiest way to learn irregular plurals is to use them and say them aloud to yourself. Here are some common examples:

SINGULAR	PLURAL	SINGULAR	PLURAL
child	children	ox	oxen
foot	feet	person	people
goose	geese	tooth	teeth
man	men	woman	women
mouse	mice		

Other irregular plurals follow certain patterns.

NOUNS ENDING IN -Y. Usually, to make these nouns plural, you change the *y* to *ie* and add -*s*.

ci**ty** + s = cit**ies**

la**dy** + s = lad**ies**

However, when a vowel (*a, e, i, o,* or *u*) comes before the *y*, just add a final -*s*.

boy + s = boys

day + s = days

NOUNS ENDING IN -F OR -FE. Usually, to make these nouns plural, you change the *f* to *v* and add -*es* or -*s*.

li**fe** + s = li**ves**

shel**f** + es = shel**ves**

thie**f** + es = thie**ves**

EXCEPTIONS: *cliffs, beliefs, roofs.*

HYPHENATED NOUNS. Sometimes, two or three words are joined with hyphens (-) to form a single noun. Usually, the *-s* is added to the first word.

attorney-at-law + s = attorneys-at-law

commander-in-chief + s = commanders-in-chief

runner-up + s = runners-up

Check a Spelling List

The following is a list of one hundred commonly misspelled words. Check this list as you proofread your writing.

One Hundred Commonly Misspelled Words

absence	career	environment	independent
achieve	category	especially	interest
across	chief	exaggerate	jewelry
aisle	column	excellent	judgment
a lot	coming	exercise	knowledge
already	commitment	fascinate	license
analyze	conscious	February	lightning
answer	convenient	finally	loneliness
appetite	cruelty	foreign	marriage
argument	daughter	friend	meant
athlete	definite	government	muscle
awful	describe	grief	necessary
basically	dictionary	guidance	ninety
beautiful	different	harass	noticeable
beginning	disappoint	height	occasion
believe	dollar	humorous	occurrence
business	eighth	illegal	perform
calendar	embarrass	immediately	physically

prejudice	rhythm	sophomore	vacuum
probably	roommate	succeed	valuable
psychology	schedule	successful	vegetable
receive	scissors	surprise	weight
recognize	secretary	truly	weird
recommend	separate	until	writing
restaurant	sincerely	usually	written

PRACTICE 8

Edit spelling errors in the following paragraph. One sentence is correct; write **C** next to it.

1 The Channel Tunnel, or Chunnel, is the rail tunnel connectting England and France. **2** Requireing ten individual contractors and thousands of workers, it was a challengeing project. **3** To complete this huge construction, a partnership had to be formed between two countrys with different languages, goverments, and sets of laws and safety codes. **4** England was definitly the more difficult country of the two. **5** For yeares, it had viewed itself as a seperate country from the rest of Europe. **6** It wanted to remain distinct, and this new connection to Europe made many English people uncomfortable. **7** Nevertheless, others saw the Chunnel as one of the best wayes to truely bring together the two countries. **8** Financeing the project was another one of the bigest obstacles. **9** The Chunnel cost billions of dollares, averaging $5 million each day of construction. **10** Ultimately, it cost seven hundred times more to develope than the Golden Gate Bridge in San Francisco, California.

15

Punctuation and Capitalization

Commas

A **comma (,)** is a punctuation mark that separates words and word groups to help readers understand a sentence. Read the following sentences, pausing when there is a comma. How does the use of commas change the meaning?

NO COMMA	When **you** call Alicia I will leave the house.
ONE COMMA	When **you** call Alicia, I will leave the house.
TWO COMMAS	When **you** call, Alicia, I will leave the house.

COMMAS BETWEEN ITEMS IN A SERIES

Use commas to separate three or more items in a series. The last item usually has *and* or *or* before it, and this joining word should be preceded by a comma.

item **,** item **,** item **,** and / or item

I put away my winter *sweaters, scarves, gloves,* **and** *hats.*

The candidates *walked to the stage, stood behind their microphones,* **and** *began yelling at each other.*

Some writers leave out the comma before the final item in a series, but doing so can lead to confusion or misreading. In college writing, it is best to include this comma.

INCORRECT

I bought bread milk and bananas.

Dan will cook I will clean and Dara will do the laundry.

Tara likes to bike, and run.

CORRECT

I bought bread, milk, and bananas.

Dan will cook, I will clean, and Dara will do the laundry.

Tara likes to bike and run.

[No comma is necessary because there are only two items.]

PRACTICE 1

In the following sentences, underline the items in the series. Then, add commas where they are needed. One sentence is correct; write **C** next to it.

> **EXAMPLE:** At the moment, I am <u>typing on my computer</u>, <u>listening to music</u>, and <u>talking on the phone</u>; doing more than one thing is called multitasking.

1. Multitasking is easier than ever thanks to gadgets such as cell phones laptop computers and portable music players.

2. People today feel the need to do two things or even three things at once.

3. I get nervous when I see someone driving talking and applying makeup at the same time.

4. I try to avoid using my cell phone while driving eating or seeing a movie.

5. Do you believe that multitasking is useful simply annoying or downright dangerous?

COMMAS IN COMPOUND SENTENCES

TIP The words *and, but, for, nor, or, so,* and *yet* are called coordinating conjunctions (see Chapter 7).

A **compound sentence** contains two sentences joined by one of these words: *and, but, for, nor, or, so, yet.* Use a comma before the joining word to separate the two clauses.

| Sentence 1 | **,** | *and, but, for, nor, or, so, yet* | sentence 2 |

The toddler knocked over the oatmeal bowl**,** **and** then she rubbed the mess into her hair.

I love my criminal justice course**,** **but** the tests are difficult.

You will not be at the meeting**,** **so** I will tell you what we decide.

INCORRECT

Jess is good with numbers and she is a hard worker.

Manuel hates to swim yet he wants to live by the water.

I meant to go, but could not.

TIP For a review of compound sentences, see Chapter 8.

CORRECT

Jess is good with numbers**,** and she is a hard worker.

Manuel hates to swim**,** yet he wants to live by the water.

I meant to go but could not.

[This sentence is not a compound, so a comma should not be used. *I meant to go* is a sentence, but *could not* is not a sentence.]

· ·

PRACTICE 2

Edit the following compound sentences by adding commas where they are needed. One sentence is correct; write **C** next to it.

EXAMPLE: Companies today realize the importance of diversity, but

prejudice still exists in the workplace.

1. Researchers recently conducted a survey of 623 American workers and the results revealed some alarming statistics.

2. Some respondents had been victims of prejudice over the previous year or they had overheard others making intolerant statements.

3. Nearly 30 percent of respondents said that they had overheard statements of racial prejudice at their workplace, and 20 percent said that coworkers had made fun of others because of their sexual orientation.

4. Age discrimination is another problem for 20 percent of respondents reported prejudice against older workers.

5. The American workforce is more diverse than ever before and it will become even more diverse in the future.

COMMAS WITH INTRODUCTORY WORDS, APPOSITIVES, AND INTERRUPTERS

Putting a comma after introductory words lets your readers know when the main part of the sentence is starting.

> Introductory word or word group **,** main part of sentence.

INTRODUCTORY WORD   *Luckily,* they got out of the burning building.

INTRODUCTORY PHRASE   *Until now,* I had never seen a ten-pound frog.

INTRODUCTORY CLAUSE   *As I explained,* Jacob eats only red jelly beans.

TIP Introductory clauses start with dependent words (subordinating conjunctions). For a review of these types of clauses, see Chapter 8.

An **appositive**, a phrase that renames a noun, comes directly before or after the noun.

> Noun **,** appositive **,** rest of sentence.

TIP For more on nouns, see Chapter 7.

Claire, *my best friend,* sees every movie starring Johnny Depp.
[*My best friend* renames *Claire.*]

You should go to Maxwell's, *the new store that opened downtown.*
[*The new store that opened downtown* renames *Maxwell's.*]

An **interrupter** is a word or word group that interrupts a sentence yet does not affect the meaning of the sentence.

> Main part of sentence **,** interrupter not essential to meaning **,** rest of sentence.

The baby, *as you know,* screams the moment I put her to bed.

Mitch hit his tenth home run of the season, *if you can believe it.*

Putting commas around appositives and interrupters tells readers that these words are not essential to the meaning of a sentence. If an appositive or interrupter is in the middle of a sentence, put a comma before and after it.

Your pants, *by the way,* are ripped.

If an appositive or interrupter comes at the beginning or end of a sentence, separate it from the rest of the sentence with one comma.

By the way, your pants are ripped.

Your pants are ripped, *by the way.*

Sometimes, appositives and interrupters are essential to the meaning of a sentence. When a sentence would not have the same meaning without the appositive, the appositive *should not* be set off with commas.

| Noun | interrupter essential to meaning | rest of sentence. |

The former seamstress *Rosa Parks* became one of the nation's greatest civil rights figures.

[The sentence *The former seamstress became one of the nation's greatest civil rights figures* does not have the same meaning.]

INCORRECT

The actor, Marlon Brando, was secretive.

Lila the best singer in my high school class is starring in a play.

He wore a clown suit to work believe it or not.

CORRECT

The actor Marlon Brando was secretive.

Lila, the best singer in my high school class, is starring in a play.

He wore a clown suit to work, believe it or not.

PRACTICE 3

Underline any appositives and interrupters in the following sentences. Then, use commas to set them off as needed.

> **EXAMPLE:** One of my favorite local shops is Melville's, a used book
>
> store.

1. I once found a rare book on collecting antique glassware my favorite hobby.

2. My favorite part of the shop the basement is dimly lit and particularly quiet.

3. A bare lightbulb the only source of light hangs from a long cord.

4. The dim light is bad for my eyes of course but it gives the basement a cozy feel.

5. Melville's is closing next month sadly because a chain bookstore around the corner has taken away much of its business.

COMMAS AROUND ADJECTIVE CLAUSES

An **adjective clause** is a group of words that

- often begins with *who, which,* or *that*
- has a subject and verb
- describes the noun right before it in a sentence

If an adjective clause can be taken out of a sentence without completely changing the meaning, put commas around the clause.

| Noun | , | adjective clause not essential to meaning | , | rest of sentence. |

The governor, *who is finishing his first term in office,* will probably not be reelected.

Devane's, *which is the best bakery in the city,* is opening two more stores.

If an adjective clause is essential to the meaning of a sentence, do not put commas around it. You can tell whether a clause is essential by taking it out and seeing if the meaning of the sentence changes significantly.

> Noun   adjective clause essential to meaning   rest of sentence.

TIP For more on adjectives, see Chapters 7 and 13.

Homeowners *who put their trash out too early* will be fined.

The jobs *that open up first* will be the first ones we fill.

Use *who* to refer to a person; *which* to refer to places or things (but not to people); and *that* to refer to people, places, or things.

INCORRECT

I like chess *which I learned to play as a child.*

The house, *that you like,* is up for sale.

Clive *who lives next door* grew a one-hundred-pound pumpkin.

CORRECT

I like chess, *which I learned to play as a child.*

The house *that you like* is up for sale.

Clive, *who lives next door,* grew a one-hundred-pound pumpkin.

PRACTICE 4

In the following sentences, underline the adjective clauses. Then, add commas where they are needed. One sentence is correct; write **C** next to it.

    EXAMPLE: Chicago's newest sushi restaurant, which I read about in a magazine, offers some unusual dishes.

1. The restaurant's dishes which look like sushi are made of paper.

2. The restaurant's chef who is interested in technology makes images of sushi dishes on an ink-jet printer.

3. He prints the images on paper that people can eat.

4. The edible paper which tastes much like sushi is flavored with food-based inks.

. . . .

COMMAS WITH QUOTATION MARKS

Quotation marks (" ") are used to show that you are repeating exactly what someone said or wrote. Generally, use commas to set off the words inside quotation marks from the rest of the sentence. Notice the position of the commas in the following dialogue:

> "Pardon me," said a stranger who stopped me on the street.
>
> "Can you tell me," he asked, "where Newland Bank is?"
>
> I replied, "Yes, you are standing right in front of it."

TIP For more on quotation marks, see pages 224–27.

COMMAS IN ADDRESSES

Use commas to separate the parts of an address included in a sentence. However, do not use a comma before a zip code.

> My address is 421 Elm Street, Burgettstown, PA 15021.

If a sentence continues after the address, put a comma after the address. Also, when you include a city and a state in the middle of a sentence, use commas before and after the state name. If the state name is at the end of a sentence, put a period after it.

> We moved from Nashville, Tennessee, to Boulder, Colorado.

COMMAS IN DATES

Separate the day from the year with a comma. If you give only the month and year, do not separate them with a comma.

> The coupon expires on May 31, 2012.
>
> I have a doctor's appointment in December 2012.

If a sentence continues after a date that includes the day, put a comma after the date.

> My grandmother was born on October 31, 1935, not far from where she lives now.

COMMAS WITH NAMES

When a sentence "speaks" to someone by name, use a comma (or commas) to separate the name from the rest of the sentence.

> Maria, could you please come here?

> Luckily, Stan, the tickets have not sold out.

> You can sit here, Phuong.

COMMAS WITH *YES* OR *NO*

Put commas around the word *yes* or *no* in response to a question or comment.

> Yes, I understand.

> I decided, no, I would not have any more soda.

PRACTICE 5

Add or delete commas as needed in the following paragraphs. Two sentences are correct; write **C** next to them.

1 When you first look up at the skyline of Malmö Sweden you might think that you are dreaming. **2** You must be imagining the building, that looks like it came from the future. **3** However you pinch yourself and find that you are wide awake. **4** The strange building which is real is one of the world's most unusual skyscrapers.

5 On Saturday, August 27 2005, a different kind of apartment building joined Malmö's skyline. **6** Built by Santiago Calatrava a Spanish architect the building is nicknamed the "Turning Torso." **7** Over six hundred feet tall the Torso is made of nine stacked cubes. **8** What makes the building particularly unusual, however is that each of these cubes is slightly turned. **9** There is a full ninety-degree twist between the top, and the bottom of the building. **10** It looks like a giant hand reached down and gave the building a powerful turn. **11** The design is based on one of Calatrava's sculptures. **12** In the sculpture he shaped a human body twisting from head to toe.

13 Already Calatrava's building has won several awards. **14** "There was a wish to get something exceptional" he told the media. **15** He added "I also wanted to deliver something technically unique." **16** The people, who choose to live in one of the building's apartments, will certainly have great views. **17** Monthly rent payments are as high as $3,700 so the experience of living in the "Turning Torso" is not for everyone.

Apostrophes

An **apostrophe (')** is a punctuation mark that

- shows ownership: *Susan's* shoes, *Alex's* coat

OR

- shows that a letter (or letters) has been left out of two words that have been joined: *I + am = I'm; that + is = that's; they + are = they're.* The joined words are called *contractions.*

Although an apostrophe looks like a comma (,), it has a different purpose, and it is written higher on the line than a comma is.

apostrophe'   comma,

APOSTROPHES TO SHOW OWNERSHIP

- **Add -'s to a singular noun to show ownership even if the noun already ends in -s.**

  The president's speech was shown on every television station.

  The suspect's abandoned car was found in the woods.

  Travis's strangest excuse for missing work was that his pet lobster died.

- **If a noun is plural (meaning *more than one*) and ends in -s, just add an apostrophe to show ownership. If it is plural but does not end in -s, add -'s.**

  TIP For more on nouns, see Chapter 7.

  Why would someone steal the campers' socks?
  [There is more than one camper.]

  The salesclerk told me where the girls' shoe department was.

  Men's hairstyles are getting shorter.

- **The placement of an apostrophe makes a difference in meaning.**

  My brother's ten dogs went to a kennel over the holiday.
  [One brother has ten dogs.]

  My brothers' ten dogs went to a kennel over the holiday.
  [Two or more brothers together have ten dogs.]

■ **Do not use an apostrophe to form the plural of a noun.**

The fan/s were silent as the pitcher wound up for the throw.

Horse/s lock their legs so that they can sleep standing up.

■ **Do not use an apostrophe with a possessive pronoun. These pronouns already show ownership (possession).**

My motorcycle is faster than your/s.

That shopping cart is our/s.

TIP For more on pronouns, see Chapters 7 and 13.

Possessive Pronouns			
my	his	its	their
mine	her	our	theirs
your	hers	ours	whose
yours			

Its or *It's*

The most common error with apostrophes and pronouns is confusing *its* (a possessive pronoun) with *it's* (a contraction meaning "it is"). Whenever you write *it's*, test to see if it is correct by reading it aloud as *it is*.

APOSTROPHES IN CONTRACTIONS

A **contraction** is formed by joining two words and leaving out one or more of the letters.

Wilma's always the loudest person in the room.
[*Wilma is* always the loudest person in the room.]

I'll babysit so that you can go to the mechanic.
[*I will* babysit so that you can go to the mechanic.]

When writing a contraction, put an apostrophe where the letter or letters have been left out, not between the two words.

He does/n't understand the risks of smoking.

Avoid contractions in formal papers for college. Some instructors believe that contractions are too informal for college writing.

Common Contractions

aren't = are not	it's = it is, it has
can't = cannot	let's = let us
couldn't = could not	she'd = she would, she had
didn't = did not	she'll = she will
don't = do not	she's = she is, she has
he'd = he would, he had	there's = there is
he'll = he will	they're = they are
he's = he is, he has	who's = who is, who has
I'd = I would, I had	won't = will not
I'll = I will	wouldn't = would not
I'm = I am	you'll = you will
I've = I have	you're = you are
isn't = is not	you've = you have

PRACTICE 6

Edit the following paragraph, adding or deleting apostrophes as needed. One sentence is correct; write **C** next to it.

1 During this course, youll be given four tests and eight quizzes. **2** The point's from those exams will make up one-half of your overall grade. **3** You are allowed to take two makeup exams during the courses duration. **4** Please do'nt ask for more than that; there will be no exceptions. **5** The other half of your grade will consist of point's for attendance, participation, homework, and two research papers. **6** All students papers and weekly homework must be turned in on time for full credit. **7** If you turn in others work as your's, you will have to leave the class. **8** Perfect attendance will earn 20 points, while 1 point will be taken off for each days absence. **9** Tutors will be available for help outside of class. **10** The research paper will be discussed four weeks before it's due date. **11** Even if you don't get a perfect average, I hope this class will be a rewarding experience.

Quotation Marks

Quotation marks (" ") are used around **direct quotations**: someone's speech or writing repeated exactly, word for word.

> **DIRECT QUOTATION**   Ellis said, "I'll finish the work by Tuesday."

Quotation marks are not used around **indirect quotations**: restatements of what someone said or wrote, not word for word.

> **INDIRECT QUOTATION**   Ellis said that he would finish the work by Tuesday.

QUOTATION MARKS FOR DIRECT QUOTATIONS

When you write a direct quotation, use quotation marks around the quoted words. These marks tell readers that the words used are exactly what was said or written.

1. "Did you hear about Carmela's date?" Rob asked me.
2. "No," I replied. "What happened?"
3. "According to Carmela," Rob said, "the guy showed up at her house in a black mask and cape."
4. I said, "You're joking, right?"
5. "No," Rob answered. "Apparently, the date thought his costume was romantic and mysterious."

Quoted words are usually combined with words that identify who is speaking, such as *Rob asked me* in the first example. The identifying words can come after the quoted words (example 1), before them (example 4), or in the middle (examples 2, 3, and 5). Here are some guidelines for capitalization and punctuation:

- Capitalize the first letter in a complete sentence that is being quoted, even if it comes after some identifying words (example 4).
- Do not capitalize the first letter in a quotation if it is not the first word in a complete sentence (*the* in example 3).
- If it is a complete sentence and its source is clear, you can let a quotation stand on its own, without any identifying words (example 5, second sentence).
- Attach identifying words to a quotation; these identifying words cannot be a sentence on their own.

- Use commas to separate any identifying words from quoted words in the same sentence.
- Always put quotation marks after commas and periods. Put quotation marks after question marks and exclamation points if they are part of the quoted sentence.

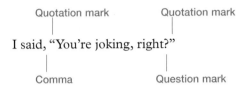

I said, "You're joking, right?"

If a question mark or exclamation point is part of your own sentence, put it after the quotation mark.

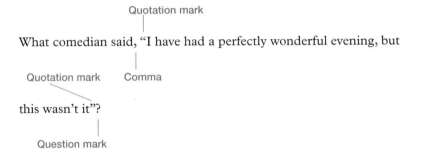

What comedian said, "I have had a perfectly wonderful evening, but

this wasn't it"?

NO QUOTATION MARKS FOR INDIRECT QUOTATIONS

When you report what someone said or wrote but do not use the person's exact words, you are writing an indirect quotation. Do not use quotation marks for indirect quotations. Indirect quotations often begin with the word *that*.

INDIRECT QUOTATION

The man asked me how to get to the store.

Martino told me that he loves me.

Carla said that she won the lottery.

DIRECT QUOTATION

The man asked me, "How do I get to the store?"

"I love you," Martino whispered in my ear.

"I won the lottery!" Carla said.

QUOTATION MARKS FOR CERTAIN TITLES

When referring to a short work such as a magazine or newspaper article, a chapter in a book, a short story, an essay, a song, or a poem, put quotation marks around the title of the work.

NEWSPAPER ARTICLE	"City Disaster Plan Revised"
SHORT STORY	"The Swimmer"
ESSAY	"A Brother's Murder"

Usually, titles of longer works—such as novels, books, magazines, newspapers, Web sites, movies, television programs, and CDs—are italicized. The titles of sacred books such as the Bible and the Qu'ran are neither underlined, italicized, nor surrounded by quotation marks.

BOOK	*The House on Mango Street*
NEWSPAPER	*Washington Post*
	[Do not underline, italicize, or capitalize the word *the* before the name of a newspaper or magazine, even if it is part of the title: **I saw that in the *New York Times*.** However, do capitalize and italicize *The* when it is the first word in titles of books, movies, and other sources.]
WEB SITE	*Facebook*

NOTE: When you write a paper for class, do not put quotation marks around the paper's title.

. . . .

PRACTICE 7

Add or delete quotation marks as needed in the following paragraph. Commas may also need to be added. Two sentences are correct; write **C** next to them.

1 You may know Orville and Wilbur Wright for their famous accomplishment: inventing and flying the world's first airplane. **2** Did you know, however, that they "began their careers as bicycle repairmen?" **3** As the newly invented bicycle began to sweep the nation, the brothers opened a repair shop because "they wanted to make sure people kept their new mode of transportation in good shape." **4** However, they later admitted that "working with bicycles kept them satisfied for only a short time." **5** As Wilbur wrote in a letter to a friend, The boys of the Wright family are all lacking in determination and push. **6** In search of a new hobby, Wilbur wrote a letter to the Smithsonian Institution and said that "he needed some information." **7** I have some pet theories as to the proper construction of a flying machine, he wrote. **8** I wish to avail myself of all that is already known and then, if possible, add my knowledge to help the future worker who will attain final success. **9** He reassured the experts at the Smithsonian that "he and his brother were serious," not just simply curious. **10** "I am an enthusiast, but not a crank," he added. **11** Even so, the brothers likely had no idea that they were close to achieving fame in aviation.

Semicolon ;

Use a semicolon to join two closely related sentences and make them into one sentence.

Sentence 1   Sentence 2

My mother warned me that being a parent is not easy; I have come to understand this.

TIP To do this chapter, you need to know what a complete sentence is. For a review, see Chapter 8.

Use semicolons to separate items in a list that themselves contain commas. Otherwise, it is difficult for readers to tell where one item ends and another begins.

We drove through Pittsburgh, Pennsylvania; Columbus, Ohio; and Indianapolis, Indiana.

Colon :

Use a colon to introduce a list after a complete sentence.

Complete sentence   List

It is impossible to escape three unpleasant facts of life: death, taxes, and strangers' cell phone conversations.

Use a colon after a complete sentence that introduces an explanation or example. If the explanation or example is also a complete sentence, capitalize the first letter after the colon.

Complete sentence   Explanation capitalized
as introduction   (complete sentence)

The refrigerator is empty: Our new roommate loves to eat.

NOTE: A colon must follow a complete sentence. A common error is to place a colon after a phrase that includes *such as* or *for example*.

INCORRECT

Shara likes winter sports, such as: skiing, ice hockey, and snowshoeing.

CORRECT

Shara likes winter sports: skiing, ice hockey, and snowshoeing.

OR

Shara likes winter sports, such as skiing, ice hockey, and snowshoeing.

Use a colon after a greeting in a business letter and after the headings at the beginning of a memorandum. (Memos are used to share information within many businesses.)

Dear Ms. Ramirez:

To: All employees

From: Mira Cole

Colons are also used between the main title and subtitle of publications.

The book that Doug read is called *Technicolor: Race, Technology, and Everyday Life.*

Parentheses   ( )

Use parentheses to set off information that is not essential to the meaning of a sentence. Do not overuse parentheses. When you do use them, they should be in pairs.

My favorite dessert (and also the most difficult one to make) is cherry strudel.

The twins have stopped arguing (at least for now) about who should get the car on Saturday.

Dash   —

Use dashes as you use parentheses: to set off additional information, particularly information that you want to emphasize.

The test — worth 30 percent of your final grade — will have forty questions.

Over the holiday, the police officers gave huge tickets — some as much as \$300 — to speeders.

A dash can also indicate a pause, much as a comma does but somewhat more forcefully.

I want to go on vacation — alone.

To make a dash, type two hyphens together, and your word processing program will automatically convert them to a dash. Alternatively, you can insert a dash as a symbol. Do not leave any extra spaces around a dash.

Hyphen   -

Use a hyphen to join words that together form a single description of a person, place, thing, or idea.

The fourteen-year-old actor went to school while making the movie.

The senator flew to Africa on a fact-finding mission.

When will the company file its year-end report?

Use a hyphen to divide a word when part of the word must continue on the next line. Most word processing programs do this automatically, but if you are writing by hand, you need to insert hyphens yourself.

At the recycling station, you will be asked to separate newspapers from aluminum cans and glass.

If you are not sure where to break a word, look it up in a dictionary. The word's main entry will show you where you can break the word: *dic-tio-nary*. If you still are not sure that you are putting the hyphen in the right place, do not break the word; write it all on the next line.

PRACTICE 8

Edit the following paragraph by adding or deleting punctuation as needed. One sentence is correct; write **C** next to it.

1 What caused Hermann Rorschach to look at ink spilled on paper and see it as a way to test people's mental health is a mystery, there is little doubt, however, that his invention is useful. **2** Created almost a century ago; these inkblots are still being used by psychiatrists today. **3** When patients look at the inkblots, they see different patterns often, things that are quite unusual.

4 One psychiatrist wrote about a varied list of things seen by just one patient, animals, buildings, people, insects, and food. **5** Psychiatrists are trained to pay attention not only to the things patients see but also to how the patients describe what they see. **6** Both are quite telling about what is going on in the patient's mind at least that is what many experts believe. **7** Psychiatrists use the inkblots to help diagnose mental illnesses: such as schizophrenia, obsessive-compulsive disorder, and multiple-personality disorder. **8** The low tech inkblots can also reveal concerns, fears, and other personality traits. **9** Sadly, the man who came up with this unique testing method did not live long enough (to see it become widely used). **10** In 1922, he died at a relatively young age thirty-seven, shortly after he published findings about his inkblots. **11** We have him to thank for an important improvement in psychiatry, a better understanding of people's mental states.

Capitalization

Capital letters are generally bigger than lowercase letters, and they may have a different form.

CAPITAL LETTERS: A, B, C, D, E, F, G, H, I, J, K, L, M, N, O, P, Q, R, S, T, U, V, W, X, Y, Z

LOWERCASE LETTERS: a, b, c, d, e, f, g, h, i, j, k, l, m, n, o, p, q, r, s, t, u, v, w, x, y, z

Capitalize (use capital letters for) the first letter of

- every new sentence
- names of specific people, places, dates, and things
- important words in titles

CAPITALIZATION OF SENTENCES

TIP To do this chapter, you need to know what a sentence is. For a review, see Chapter 8.

Capitalize the first letter of each new sentence, including the first word in a direct quotation.

The police officer broke up our noisy party.

He said, "Do you realize how loud your music is?"

CAPITALIZATION OF NAMES OF SPECIFIC PEOPLE, PLACES, DATES, AND THINGS

Capitalize the first letter in names of specific people, places, dates, and things (also known as proper nouns). Do not capitalize general words such as *college* as opposed to the specific name: *Witley College.*

PEOPLE

Capitalize the first letter in names of specific people and in titles used with names of specific people.

SPECIFIC	NOT SPECIFIC
Patty Wise	my friend
Dr. Jackson	the physician
President Barack H. Obama	the president
Professor Arroyo	your professor
Aunt Marla, Mother	my aunt, my mother

The name of a family member is capitalized when the family member is being addressed directly or when the family title is replacing a first name.

Sit down here, Sister.

I wish Mother would see a doctor.

In other cases, do not capitalize.

My sister came to the party.

I am glad that my mother is seeing a doctor.

PLACES

Capitalize the first letter in names of specific buildings, streets, cities, states, regions, and countries.

SPECIFIC	NOT SPECIFIC
the Seagram Building	that building
Elm Street	our street
Jacksonville, Florida	my town
Wisconsin	this state
the South	the southern part of the country
Chinatown	my neighborhood
Pakistan	her birthplace

Do not capitalize directions in a sentence: *Drive north for three miles.*

DATES

Capitalize the first letter in the names of days, months, and holidays. Do not capitalize the names of the seasons (winter, spring, summer, fall).

SPECIFIC	NOT SPECIFIC
Friday	today
July	summer
Martin Luther King Jr. Day	my birthday

ORGANIZATIONS, COMPANIES, AND SPECIFIC GROUPS

SPECIFIC	NOT SPECIFIC
Doctors Without Borders	the charity
Starbucks	the coffee shop
Wilco	his favorite band

LANGUAGES, NATIONALITIES, AND RELIGIONS

SPECIFIC	NOT SPECIFIC
English, Spanish, Chinese	my first language
Christianity, Islam	her religion

The names of languages should be capitalized even if you are not referring to a specific course: I am studying economics and French.

COURSES

SPECIFIC	NOT SPECIFIC
English 100	a writing course
Psychology 100	the introductory psychology course

COMMERCIAL PRODUCTS

SPECIFIC	NOT SPECIFIC
Nikes	sneakers
Tylenol	pain reliever

CAPITALIZATION OF TITLES

Capitalize the first word and all other important words in titles of books, movies, television programs, magazines, newspapers, articles, stories, songs, papers, poems, and so on. Words that do not need to be capitalized (unless they are the first or last word) include *the, a,* and *an;* the conjunctions *and, but, for, nor, or, so,* and *yet;* and prepositions.

TIP For a list of common prepositions, see page 90.

> *American Idol* is Marion's favorite television show.
>
> Did you read the article titled "Humans Should Travel to Mars"?
>
> We read *The Awakening,* a novel by Kate Chopin.

PRACTICE 9

Edit the following paragraph by capitalizing words as needed or by deleting unnecessary capital letters. One sentence is correct; write **C** next to it.

1 This first unit of American History 101 will focus on the civil rights movement. **2** We will explore this movement from the Civil War until Current times. **3** Six of the eight weeks devoted to this unit will concentrate on the 1960s, when struggles for Civil Rights made daily headlines across the Nation. **4** we will learn about leaders such as Martin Luther King Jr., Rosa Parks, Malcolm X, and jesse jackson. **5** We will also examine the history of the Ku Klux Klan, the development of the National association for the advancement of Colored People, and the passage of the Civil Rights act of 1964. **6** As we work through the material, you will be given reading assignments from your textbook, *the American promise*. **7** A final exam covering the course material will be given on december 15 in howard hall. **8** Tutoring in this unit will be available through my Teaching assistants, Ms. Chambers and Mr. Carlin. **9** If you have any questions, please see me after class or during my Office Hours.

Photo Credits

Page 8. Let's Move! Campaign screenshot. Courtesy of letsmove.gov.

Page 9. Drunk driving public service announcement. Courtesy of the U.S. Department of Transportation, on behalf of the Ad Council.

Index

Four Basics of Good Writing

1 It achieves the writer's purpose.

2 It considers the readers (the audience).

3 It includes a main point.

4 It has details that support the main point.

2PR   The Critical Reading Process

Preview the reading.

Read the piece, finding the main point and support.

Pause to think during reading. Ask yourself questions about what you are reading. Imagine that you are talking to the author.

Review the reading, your notes, and your questions. Build your vocabulary by looking up any unfamiliar words.